IT'S ONLY A GAME

Darrel Johnson

Copyright ©2025 by Darrel Johnson (Higher Ground Books & Media)
All rights reserved. No part of this publication may be reproduced in any form, stored in a retrieval system, or transmitted in any form, or by any means (electronic, mechanical, photocopying, recording or otherwise) without prior permission by the copyright owner and the publisher of this book.

Scripture taken from the HOLY BIBLE, NEW INTERNATIONAL VERSION®. NIV®. Copyright © 1973, 1978, 1984 by International Bible Society. Used by permission of Zondervan. All rights reserved worldwide.

Higher Ground Books & Media
Springfield, OH 45501-2914
www.highergroundbooksandmedia.com

Because of the dynamic nature of the Internet, any web addresses or links contained in this book may have changed since publication and may no longer be valid. The views expressed in the work are solely those of the author and do not necessarily reflect the views of the publisher, and the publisher hereby disclaims any responsibility for them.

Any people depicted in stock imagery are being used for illustrative purposes only.

ISBN (Paperback): 978-1-955368-88-9

Printed in the United States of America 2025

IT'S ONLY A GAME

Darrel Johnson

To Derek and Lauren, who have shown me that the closest thing we will ever know to God's love is a father's love for his children. May He always guide your paths.

"I have no greater joy than to hear that my children are walking in the truth."
3 John 1:4

TABLE OF CONTENTS

4   Foreword - Bill Self (Head Basketball Coach, University of Kansas)
5   Preface
6   Introduction

Chapter 1	An Innocent Man
Chapter 2	Beyond the Scoreboard
Chapter 3	The New Chief
Chapter 4	Odd Man Out
Chapter 5	The Pursuit of a Superstar
Chapter 6	Seeking Justice
Chapter 7	Down to Business
Chapter 8	Hail to the Chiefs
Chapter 9	Bad to the Bone
Chapter 10	The Boycott
Chapter 11	The Investigation
Chapter 12	Indicted
Chapter 13	The Trial
Chapter 14	The Verdict
Chapter 15	Broken
Chapter 16	Trust the Nudge
Chapter 17	Where is God?
Chapter 18	Changing the Culture
Chapter 19	Back-to-Back (Again)
Chapter 20	The Buzzer Sounds
Chapter 21	Reflections

FOREWORD

Darrel Johnson was my assistant coach at Oklahoma State University and became a basketball lifer as a college coach and NBA scout. But his story is more than just about the game itself and winning games and championships. It's also a story about rising out of difficult circumstances and persevering through trials. Darrel is using his story to inspire and help others when the journey seems too long and too hard. It certainly has impacted me. This read is about hope, faith, inspiration and a road map for the trip to live a purposeful life.

Bill Self
Head Basketball Coach
University of Kansas

PREFACE

It's hard to believe that it's been thirty years. Finally in early 2024 one of my former college players invited me to a retired coach's luncheon, sponsored by long time Oklahoma FCA director, John O'Dell. I resisted, but he kept asking. Finally, I caved and went. I had not seen O'Dell in over 25 years since I was a high school coach in Oklahoma. But we quickly reconnected like we had never lost touch. And before I left that day, he asked me to speak to the group at a future luncheon. I agreed to it but had no idea what to talk about. That is until I felt an overwhelming conviction … that God was moving me to tell my story. It wasn't a voice but more like a nudge, or maybe even a push. God was telling me it was time to share the story that He had given me. My good friend Kent Shellenberger attended the luncheon when I first spoke about the biggest battle I've ever fought. He had never heard it before, but neither had anyone else. I sat on it for thirty years before I felt the stirring to go public. Kent urged me to keep telling it. People need to hear this, he said, because at some point in our life, we all must persevere after going through pain and struggling with our faith. So here we are. I held it in for three decades because of the shame, the embarrassment, the pain, and the most public humiliation imaginable. But it's been therapeutic, and I believe the average sports fan and general public can relate and are more forgiving than I could possibly give them credit. The story seems to resonate since I've been asked numerous times to speak since that first time in January 2024. It seems others can identify, and it finally occurred to me that we're all interested in other people's stories, maybe because we ALL have a story to tell. The names and circumstances will differ, but many of life's battles that we all endure have startling similarities. But I cannot tell this story except in the context of my faith in Jesus Christ, who gave me the redemptive grace to recover from losing everything, to starting over, and ultimately to flourish as a child of God. For years, media types from all avenues have asked for "my side of the story." But I wasn't ready … and maybe God wasn't ready either, until now.

This is my story.

INTRODUCTION

   Being a sports fan in Oklahoma automatically meant that Mickey Mantle was a childhood hero. Baseball was my first true love and was really my only connection with my dad, who coached the Monroe Redbirds baseball team. We were good ... really good, and we were all passionate about winning. In fact, we won a Pee Wee state championship, which by the way is kind of a big deal to a nine-year-old that loves baseball. But the only school sports team offered at Taft Junior High in Oklahoma City was basketball. I tried out in seventh grade and got cut. Most of my friends made the team and I watched every game they played while vowing that I would be with them next year as an eighth grader. Not making the team was an early lesson, which paid huge dividends down the road. It taught me work ethic, that nothing worth having would ever just be given to me, and that achieving my dreams was worth my very best efforts and sacrifices. I watched, and practiced, and trained ... and grew. I was in the starting lineup the next season on a Taft team that won a city championship. My lunch hours were spent alone in the gym working on my game. I'd stay after school to get shots up, then go home and put in some extra time by myself on the driveway where my dad had saved money to put up a basketball goal. I played in every neighborhood pickup game I could find, and like most kids would fantasize about hitting the game winner to bring home the championship trophy. I remember standing in the gym during my lunch breaks at Taft, breathing in the awesomeness of what would become my lifetime dream. Oh, how I loved this game.
   After Taft, we moved on to Putnam City Central Middle School, where I set an all-time scoring record as a freshman. The next stop would be as a sophomore at Putnam City High School, the largest school in Oklahoma. I was the only sophomore to make the varsity squad and ended up becoming a starter before semester break. The team made the state tournament before losing a close game in the state semi-finals. But we were about to re-write the record books the following year.
   The 1971-72 Putnam City Pirates would become the greatest high school basketball team in Oklahoma history. The team went undefeated, won the state championship in Oklahoma's largest class, with an average victory margin of 27 points per game, a feat that has

not since been duplicated. This was of course before the days of the shot clock and the three point line in amateur basketball. But before I take any credit for this monumental accomplishment, it should be noted that the 1972 Pirates were led by a guy named Alvan Adams. Adams would eventually become the NBA Rookie of the Year in 1975 and the second leading scorer in Phoenix Suns history. In fact, any high school team with Alvan Adams would have become an instant title contender. He was that good. But this team was special, with seven players eventually playing college basketball. In this era at Putnam City High School, winning was easy. Making the team, in any sport, was the hard part. The football team was led by Steve Largent who still holds NFL receiving records with the Seattle Seahawks and is a member of the pro football hall of fame. The quarterback was Pat Ryan who went on to play at the University of Tennessee and later spent a decade with the NFL's New York Jets. The baseball team was anchored by Bob Shirley who became a star pitcher for the New York Yankees, the San Diego Padres, and the St. Louis Cardinals. And then there was Alvan, who today stands as the all-time leading rebounder in Suns history, as well as their second leading scorer behind Walter Davis. We had other guys too numerous to mention that also had stellar college careers in various sports. It's no wonder why winning was easy for us. We had so many gifted athletes, and it is still amazing that so many were in the same high school at the same time.

We fell short of a repeat state championship the next year but still had a great season and made it to the state semi-finals. Individually, I had broken Alvan's all-time single game scoring record with 44 points against Moore High School in the regular season. I was probably somewhat over recruited and went on to play at The University of Tulsa. My college career had its ups and downs but was highlighted by a victory over Louisville in 1975, who went on to play against UCLA in the Final Four. Louisville was coached by Hall of Famer Denny Crum and led by Junior Bridgeman who was later drafted by the Los Angeles Lakers in the lottery and had a stellar NBA career. There were plenty of tough times as well. Like the game against cross-town rival Oral Roberts University in 1975. The game was played at the Mabee Center on the campus of ORU. The building was only three years old and was easily the top arena in the state, and one of the best in the country. The 1975 game had all the hype one might expect for a rivalry game. Every seat in the arena was filled, with a standing room only crowd of more than 11,000 fans. At the time, it set an all-time record for the largest crowd ever to watch a college basketball game in Oklahoma. It was my junior year at Tulsa, and we had just gone through a head coaching change. Ken Hayes had recruited me out of Putnam City but was let go after my sophomore year. Jim "Country" King replaced him who had played at Tulsa and later in the NBA. His only coaching experience was being the head man for Athletes in Action, a Christian touring team that played mostly an exhibition schedule against college teams. The game with ORU came down to the wire and with ten seconds left in the game we had the ball, down by a point. King called time out and diagramed a play for me to get the ball and take the final shot. It worked to perfection, and I was fouled near the basket with one second remaining. The place was going absolutely crazy with both sides screaming at the top of their lungs. I'd shoot two free throws for a chance to win the game with .001 left on the game clock. Being a career eighty percent free throw shooter, I stepped to the line with confidence. The first shot missed off the back of the rim. I couldn't believe it; I had been automatic from the line for most of the season. Now we were looking at overtime with one made free throw. I took a deep breath, bounced it a couple of times, then let it fly. The ball rolled around the rim a couple of times before coming off and missing. We lost the game by a point which was the first loss ever for Tulsa in the rivalry game that had been dubbed as "the Mayor's Cup." It was the most traumatic point of my playing career, and one I'll never forget. It's like the kicker on the football team missing the extra point to win the game. I went into a severe depression, and it affected the rest of my year, which was mediocre at best. I transferred to Southern Nazarene University after the season and played there a year before heading overseas to play professional basketball in Manchester, England. But I never forgot that failed opportunity against ORU. Manchester was a fantastic, once-in-a-lifetime experience but after a single season it was time to come home to Oklahoma to begin a coaching career. I loved the game as much as ever and could not imagine a life without basketball. I began coaching at home in the Putnam City school system for a couple of years before landing my first head coaching job at Ada (Oklahoma) High School. Our two-season record at Ada ended at 44-11 with a state championship in 1982, a decade after winning a state title at Putnam City.

Ada was a dream job at the age of 25 and I truly thought I would be there for twenty years or longer. But a huge break came my way in 1982 after our state championship run. Paul Hansen at Oklahoma State University called and asked if I would be interested in becoming his top assistant coach. Paul and I had some history when he coached at Oklahoma City University and tried to recruit me. We became friends, but an opportunity like this at a major college rarely comes along for a high school coach. I jumped at the opportunity and joined the OSU staff. Coach Hansen became a best friend and a mentor.

My first year at Oklahoma State was Paul's best year as we won a Big 8 conference championship before losing to Princeton in the first round of the NCAA tournament. I was living my dream every day. But the best thing that came out of my job at OSU was that I met my future wife, Denna. After three years at OSU, I felt it was time to be a head coach again and I accepted the job at Oklahoma Baptist University. Denna and I married in 1985 and started a new life together in Shawnee, Oklahoma. After five years in Shawnee, I took over for Abe Lemons, who had retired as head coach at Oklahoma City University after a Hall of Fame career. OBU had been a tough job, but I was excited now about going back home to Oklahoma City. Two championship seasons at OCU opened a new door for my career path and presented an opportunity that rarely happens for a small college coach.

It was an absolute dream come true. Not just being a Division One head basketball coach but being at a program with such promise. Baylor University was the big time ...going head-to-head with some of the nation's elite basketball powers. After suffering through four straight losing seasons, it was the perfect job at the perfect time for the new coach. We turned it around quickly. We started winning. People who had become disinterested and apathetic started coming to games and buying season tickets. We led the entire nation in increased attendance, had a ranked recruiting class coming, and had two straight winning seasons. I was the toast of Waco, Texas with a new five-year contract, more money than I ever thought possible, my own TV and radio shows, and a summer camp that was bursting at the seams. Life wasn't just good ...it was great! Until it wasn't. Because in 1994 for the first time in NCAA history, a major college basketball coach was indicted by a federal grand jury charged with seven counts of federal crimes over the recruitment and eligibility of college basketball players. I was that head coach. How could this happen? Never so much as a parking ticket and I'm now looking at the possibility of years in a federal penitentiary. A career ended, a life disrupted, a family broken, and a most public humiliation. My record as a basketball coach, two national championships, teams with star-studded recruits, a history of turning around losing programs, and an impeccable reputation … none of which could save me now. Thirty years later and looking back, I was facing the toughest battle of my life. I was not just fighting for my career, my livelihood and my reputation, but now, I was also fighting for my freedom. Basketball was the one true love of my life and everything else had become incidental, including a once passionate Christian faith. This game had become my mistress, my life's passion and even my identity. But now more than ever, I needed God. But where was He in all of this? I felt let down, even betrayed by His absence. My faith was shaken, and I had lost everything. How could God let this happen? It's just basketball. And It's Only a Game.

"You shall not bear false witness against your neighbor." Exodus 20:16

CHAPTER 1 - AN INNOCENT MAN

Ladies and gentlemen of the jury, have you reached a verdict? The courtroom was silent ... all knowing that a young man's life was hanging in the balance. A year of media attention and scrutiny, as well as a long, clandestine undercover operation by Oklahoma detectives, had come down to this verdict. Calvin Moore had been a basketball star at McLennan Community College in Waco, Texas and was the brightest piece of my recruiting class in 1988 at Oklahoma Baptist University. OBU was a faith-based, Christian university in Shawnee, Oklahoma with high academic standards and a strict moral code. It was an expensive private school, and its sports programs were among those of the National Association of Interscholastic Athletics (NAIA). Their most recent men's basketball history was dismal, and I was brought in to turn things around. After three years as an assistant coach at Oklahoma State which included a Big 8 championship and NCAA tournament bid, I felt ready to be a head coach. So, when OBU came calling I accepted.

The team had been losing, graduation rates were low, and the brass at OBU was calling into question the personal character and academic readiness of many of its current players. The mandate I was given was to win games with highly academic-minded kids who demonstrated impeccable moral character. There was also an emphasis given on local recruiting (Oklahoma), and transfer students were frowned upon. And for the first two years at OBU, that's exactly what I gave them, with one notable exception. Our team GPA was through the roof, and we had an array of local kids who represented our school in a positive manner. The only problem was that we were losing badly. My first two years as a college head coach produced a record of 15 wins and 49 losses. So, I prepared myself for the inevitable when I got the call after the season to report to the President's office for a "review" of our program. I thought I was about to be fired. Dr. Bob Agee was our president. He was academic-minded, but pretty much called the shots on all personnel matters, in all departments. So, when I prepared for the meeting with

Agee, I knew I'd have to fight for my job. He knew little about the inner workings of intercollegiate athletics, but in fairness, he had to be concerned about the bottom line, our record, and how it looked to the outside world. During our meeting, I reminded him of the state of the program when I arrived ... losing records, low graduation rates, some bad actors and a team that did not represent the face of the university in a positive manner. I think that part was not lost on Agee, but near the end of our meeting, he flat out said it ... I wanna win!! Now I do think he saw that there were some positives to build on, but that record was hard to swallow. In the end, Agee reluctantly extended my contract for one more year with only one condition. We either produced a winning record, or I was gone. Nothing about character or graduation rates, just win! I agreed and breathed a sense of relief that I had one more shot to prove myself. Most pressure on coaches is self-applied, but this was different. This was the ultimate pressure situation ... win now or lose your job, and it came directly from the president himself. Our recruiting philosophy had to change despite the initial marching orders I had received from the administration. In my mind, there was no more emphasis on academics. The directive I had now was clear ... just win. And do it quickly.

So, I started a new recruiting year looking only at transfers... players with college playing experience. I no longer had the luxury of waiting on freshmen to develop. But perhaps the most important signee of the year was my new assistant coach, Win Case. I convinced Win to join me at OBU in this most critical recruiting season. I had recruited Win to Oklahoma State University from Seminole Junior College where he was our starting point guard for two years alongside Bill Self, the current and long-time Kansas coach. Win was a quality player but also an affable young man who never met a stranger. He had no experience, but I was certain he would be really good as a recruiter. And I was right. He now coaches at Southern Mississippi, but Win and I have a long history together, and he still stands out as the best recruiter and assistant coach I've ever had.

The kids I had recruited to OBU as freshmen were now older, and more experienced. And we had Calvin, who was a legitimate pro prospect. But they didn't know how to win, and I'm not sure I did either. A two-year record of 15-49 will shake the confidence of players and coaches alike. The players we had were solid, but we lacked star power. Win and I signed a couple of junior college players from Texas, Vince Alexander from Blinn and Fernando Tomasiello from Paris. Both were solid but still didn't raise our talent level enough to compete for championships. We needed a difference-maker.

Jim Kerwin was an assistant coach for Billy Tubbs at the University of Oklahoma, and before that, had coached Win at Seminole Junior College. Jim was a good friend, but he and Win were very close. Win had been his leader and team captain at Seminole, and they had an extremely high level of trust and mutual respect. Oklahoma had recruited and signed a couple of Oklahoma high school players that looked like they were going to be Prop 48 casualties. Which meant that they were not going to qualify and meet NCAA academic requirements. Non-qualifiers had limited options by NCAA rules. They could go to an NCAA school and be bound by their letter of intent but would lose their freshman year of eligibility. And to gain eligibility for the second year, the player would have to meet the school's and the NCAA's academic guidelines for satisfactory progress toward a degree. The other option, and the road most often taken, was that the player would go to a junior college, play for two years and graduate. So, either way a non-qualifier was going to lose eligibility.

But in 1987 there was a new, more uncommon approach. The player could go to a non-NCAA member institution and play his freshman year. If his grades were satisfactory, he could then transfer back to the NCAA school with 3 years of eligibility remaining. The advantages of this route were significant. A player could play his full freshman season with the understanding that he would then transfer back to the school with whom he had originally committed. So, Kerwin pitched the idea to us, that Lance Kroll and Stacey Wilson, both University of Oklahoma signees and non-qualifiers, would sign a one-year scholarship with OBU. The advantage for OU was that they would be able to watch these players compete and then decide if they wanted them back. And if they came back, it would be as more seasoned, experienced players. The downside was that neither player was obligated to honor their letter of intent with OU, so recruiting would be opened up all over again. But the same was true if they went the juco route, so Kerwin and OU head coach Billy Tubbs were willing to take that chance, with the idea of having them return with three years to play and no graduation requirement. So here were two high major college-level players that just fell in our lap. Kroll was a bruising, 6'10 center and had been ranked nationally as a top fifty recruit. And Wilson was a 6'7 elite, over-the-rim type athlete that just oozed with pro potential. Now we had our star power! And optimism was high for the upcoming season. A season that would make or break my career as a college basketball coach.

As Hall of Fame coach Al McGuire once quipped while coaching at Marquette… "the best thing about freshmen is that next year they'll be sophomores." His point is that it's really hard to win with freshmen. Kroll and Davis were both high-level division one talents, but they were still freshmen. And there was a learning curve. I didn't have time to wait for them to develop, they had to play now. My third season was tougher than we thought it would be. Our freshman didn't dominate like we had hoped, and the rest of the team was comprised of mostly role players. So, we struggled. Halfway through the season, we found ourselves in the middle of the pack in our league, hovering around the .500 mark. The winning season mandate given to me by the OBU administration was reachable, but certainly not a given. Kroll was solid but his lack of athleticism was apparent, and he wasn't prepared for the speed of the college game. Wilson thrived in up-tempo and open floor situations, but he lacked a high-level offensive skill set to make plays or score when defended by similar type athletes. So, the pressure of this season was almost unbearable. I was trying to squeeze every drop I could get out of our players, all while suffering from migraines and lack of sleep. It was not uncommon for me to pop 10-12 extra strength Tylenol every day, just trying to make it through. The job was all-consuming anyway, but with my career hanging in the balance on these next few games, the daily stress was more than I'd ever experienced. All this for a job that paid about twenty-five thousand dollars per year. But this was my chosen profession. I didn't know what I'd do if it was taken away from me. My whole life had been basketball. I had played for four years collegiately and two years professionally overseas. My first job had been as a junior high coach, then a high school assistant, then a high school head coach where we had won a state championship in Ada Oklahoma. My wife, Denna, was depending on me and she wanted to start a family. But I was on the cusp of losing my job, my income, and my career. Most coaches while in the profession don't really understand that there is actually life outside of basketball. It's all we've ever done and it's all we really know. And it's not like coaching prepares you for a lot of other vocational pathways. At least in my mind it didn't. What would I do? Where would I go, and how would I make a living?

Success as a college coach was evading me. I truly loved it ... I lived and breathed the coaching side of the game, and it was on my mind every waking moment. But why was it so hard to win? I needed to be a better coach, but in my mind more importantly, I needed better players. Our season was winding down and we didn't make the playoffs. Heading into our final game of the year we had a record of 13-13. The game meant little to our players, it would be our final game of the season win or lose. But the game meant my livelihood to me. Win our last game and hopefully, I would get another year. Lose it and I would most certainly be gone. Our final game was against USAO (University of Science and Arts of Oklahoma) which was coached by my best friend and mentor Paul Hansen. I had known Paul since he was at Oklahoma City University, as an assistant coach for the legendary Abe Lemons. Paul inherited the OCU job when Abe left to coach at Pan American and then the University of Texas. Hansen had remarkable success at OCU, enough to land the head coaching gig at Oklahoma State. In 1982 after winning a state championship at Ada High School, I got a call from Coach Hansen asking if I would be interested in being his assistant at OSU. Going from the high school ranks to being the top assistant at a high major program was almost unheard of, so I jumped at the chance. In my first year at OSU, we beat Missouri in the finals of the conference tournament to advance to the NCAA tournament. Paul was teaching me the ropes of being a college coach and recruiting. He was good at both and was one of the most beloved sports celebrities in Oklahoma. Like everyone else, I had heard all the stories about cheating in college basketball and the corruption of the sport. But Paul was squeaky clean and never had even the slightest blemish on his reputation as a college coach. He was doing things the right way and was winning. I felt like I was learning from the best. It was after three years at OSU that I felt ready to be a head coach. I had recruiting experience, division one experience, and had won a state championship in high school as a player, and later as a coach. Paul knew I had the itch to have my own program and recommended me to the OBU coaching search committee. I had a couple of other heavyweights in my corner, most notably Henry Iba, who had coached at OSU and was the Men's Basketball US Olympic coach for years. Mr. Iba was a legend in Oklahoma, and really everywhere else for anyone that knew anything about basketball. I got the job at OBU and Paul's teams took a nosedive after the championship season in 1983. He was relieved of his duties the year after I left for OBU and resurfaced at USAO where he would finish out his most distinguished basketball coaching career. And now, quite coincidentally, he was coaching the team that had the opportunity to end my career.

I spoke with Hansen before the game and told him what was riding on this game. It was not my finest moment, but the stress and pressure had taken its toll. Paul kind of laughed it off ... because the bottom line was that he wanted to win, but he also did not want me to lose. I knew it would be a tough game against my mentor and friend, and I also knew the nature of this business was to try and do everything you can do to win, even against a friend or protege.

My team at OBU was actually more talented than USAO, but they had the great equalizer ... they had a better coach. I tried to impress upon our players that we were building something here, that we were playing for a winning season, and we were playing for personal pride. The game went back and forth. Both teams competed hard, which was somewhat surprising since the outcome really didn't mean much. It was close, but in the end, we won. We completed our season at 14 and 13 ...OBU's first winning season since 1982. And I felt sure my job would now be safe, at least for another year.

The OBU President and administration were less than enthused about renewing my contract for another year. We had not made the playoffs and seemed to underachieve given our player talent level. But we had a winning season, and there was reason to be somewhat hopeful for the future, especially if we could keep our OU prop 48 stash, Kroll and Wilson. Agee again reluctantly agreed to give me another year, and I could at least breathe again. The season was less than stellar and far less than what we had hoped for. We had to get better... or the future would be inevitable, my coaching career would end at OBU. Things got worse shortly thereafter when it became apparent that Kroll and Wilson had their sights set higher than staying at OBU. OU had watched their progress during the season and was not impressed enough to recruit them again. But Kroll had managed to make his grades and signed with Wichita State University, giving him a chance at 3 years of Division One basketball. Wilson had not received any offers and ended up going the juco route, where he would need to improve his game, graduate, and then go through the recruiting process again. So, we had just finished our season one game above .500 only to lose our two best prospects for the future. And even though it wasn't totally unexpected, we had hoped to keep these guys and now faced the prospect of starting over again with a new recruiting class.

Our talent level after the defections of our OU transplants took a major hit. We had to replenish the roster with players that could make an immediate impact. We needed division-one caliber players that weren't going to go that route. We did not have the luxury of trying to find that diamond in the rough, under-the-radar types. And really that is mostly a myth talked about by those that have never been in the recruiting trenches. Every college coach knows their livelihood depends on recruiting players who can help you win. The intangibles can't be underestimated ... the ones with a great attitude, hard worker, super coachable, great teammate and so on. But that aside, we needed high-level talent. And if a player is that talented and is not going division one, there's usually a reason. Most often the reason is grades, test scores, or in the case of junior colleges, they don't graduate with a two-year degree. With no diploma in hand, junior college players are not eligible for NCAA Division One basketball. So, our direction was clear if we were going to really try and compete at a championship level. Now this was contrary to what OBU execs had said they wanted. But clearly, their way didn't work, at least it didn't with me as the head coach. But high-level junior college talents that don't graduate are the targets of most non-division one basketball programs. It's a way to gain an advantage and compete with the bigger programs. So, these players are in high demand and are heavily recruited at our level. The competition for these types of players is fierce. But we were throwing our hat into the ring.

Our first recruiting trip after the season was to McLennan Community College in Waco, Texas where Calvin Moore had just completed a spectacular sophomore year of junior college. He would be my number one target to get this program on the winning track. Calvin was listed as one of the top juco prospects in the country but was not being recruited by the Division One schools because he had no chance of graduating from MCC. He became a huge priority recruit for all non-D-1 schools that offered full scholarships.

Win and I hit the road for Waco to try and recruit Calvin Moore to OBU. Calvin was a 6'7 hybrid type that would do well in today's game. He could play multiple positions, inside and out, and had a skill set that was highly unusual for this level of college basketball. Going into his recruitment, I felt like Calvin had the potential to be the best NAIA player to ever come out of the state, which is saying something with former NBA star, Dennis Rodman, playing at Southeastern Oklahoma. Calvin was definitely a more skilled offensive player than Rodman. Win hit it off immediately with Calvin and I quickly made friends with one of the academic advisors at MCC. Calvin had been the best player for MCC, but the team as a whole was outstanding and there were other players that were being recruited. We soon understood that these guys wanted to continue their careers at the same place. So, the key to getting Calvin was to recruit the other players on the team. The truth is that they were all good enough to contribute at our level, but the real prize in the end would be Calvin. After a long courtship, an official visit by the players to our campus, and several more trips to Waco, we ended up signing Calvin Moore, Willie Gilmore, Carl Love, and Nathan McCoy, all from MCC. Anthony Booker, also from McClennan who had signed with Texas A&M, later left the school and transferred to OBU to play with his friends. So, this was the nucleus of our recruiting class and the guys we were counting on to save our job. We certainly thought we'd be good enough to compete for a league championship with this class. These players had already developed some chemistry by playing together in junior college, and they were experienced with two years of college basketball under their belts. The next and most important season of my career was just a few months away. Our roster was replenished with quality, experienced players. But the question would be how well they would fit into the OBU environment. They were all marginal students by OBU standards, none of them had graduated from MCC, and there were some strong personalities in the group. But we also signed a transfer player from Oklahoma State, William (Cookie) Woods. Cookie had been a star high school player from Oklahoma who was heavily recruited. He signed at OSU but got caught up in a coaching change and wasn't getting the playing time he wanted. Coach Case was on him from the beginning and the two had lots of common ground. Both had played high school basketball in Oklahoma, and both had played at OSU. Win convinced him that OBU would be a great landing spot. Cookie was vastly different from the JC kids we had already signed. He wanted more playing time, but he was genuinely interested in getting a solid education, which was refreshing and certainly more palatable for the OBU academic higher-ups. Cookie further solidified our recruiting class. We felt like we had drastically improved our overall talent level from last year's squad, even with the departure of Kroll and Wilson. The main question would be the fit, on campus, and how well these guys would be received. I was determined to make it a smooth transition.

Small schools like OBU do not have the luxury of elaborate academic support programs like they do at the big schools. When I was at OSU, if an athlete was having trouble in class, he would be assigned to a tutor, a counselor, and other academic support personnel. At OBU the academic support person was me. I had to stay on top of the players and their classes, or we'd most likely have some academic casualties. So, study hall supervision and academic advisement were things that just came along with the job of being the coach.

I had become friends with the local director of the Section 8 housing authority in Shawnee, who assured me that all the MCC recruits should qualify for government-subsidized, section 8 housing off campus, based on their income. This was a departure from the norm for an OBU student, but the players wanted to be off campus, and I convinced my athletic director that it was in everyone's best interest. I was obviously still concerned about how the players would be accepted by the campus community.

Win and I coached these guys hard, and we knew we had to win, but we also had to make the community comfortable with our guys. We needed their support, and we needed fans. If a player missed a class, they were disciplined. If they weren't making grades, they were assigned extra work and study hall. And if they didn't act right, there would be consequences. Most JC kids are accustomed to a loose ship, but we couldn't do that here. In addition to the academic requirements and the rigorous practice schedule, I led a voluntary Bible study once a week. The players weren't required to attend, but most of them did. We were a Baptist school with a strong foundation in the Christian faith. And it was my job to make sure our program was an extension of the school's beliefs and philosophies. I grew up a Christian, a Baptist, and it was important to me.

Calvin was brilliant the next season as we knew he would be.

He led our team in both scoring and rebounding and was named first-team all-conference. But the supporting cast was good too. The players in the program had grown up, our recruiting class was talented and experienced, and maybe I was a little better coach. We fought hard all year and competed for a championship. The team was nationally ranked for a brief time, before finishing tied for first place in our league, with an overall record of 22-9, the best record by the school in over a decade. But Agee still was not convinced that I was the right guy for the job. He deferred the decision to my athletic director as to whether or not to renew my contract for another season. I was voted league coach of the year, but Agee thought our talent level was out of this world and was still convinced we weren't reaching our fullest potential. But our athletic director, Norris Russell, had more realistic expectations and opted to renew for another year. With a league co-championship finish, a nationally ranked team, and a 22-9 record with everyone returning, next year we'd be the odds-on favorite to win a championship. We were loaded and the future looked bright.

But the off-season was full of surprises and disappointment. Not the least of which was a phone call I received in the summer of 1989. I was on a recruiting trip and had stopped off to see my good friend, Jim Wooldridge, in Warrensburg, Missouri. Jim was the head coach at Central Missouri State University and later became an assistant with the Chicago Bulls and head coach at Kansas State. We had played high school basketball together and had stayed close friends through the years... and competed with one another both on and off the court. Years later, when the coaching job at Southwest Texas State came open, Jim and I were the two finalists for the job. We interviewed on the same day, though the search committee had no idea we even knew each other. I actually was offered the job and turned it down, and Jim became the head coach, which was a huge springboard in his career. But on this particular day...a time before cell phones, the call came to Jim's house. It was my wife, Denna. Jim put the phone down ... "DJ you better take this call."

Denna had received a call from Norris Russell, my athletic director at OBU, looking for me. "Darrel, you need to get back to campus as soon as you can. Calvin Moore has been arrested for selling cocaine to an undercover police officer." My heart sank! Are you kidding me? Not only was Calvin our best player and our leading scorer and rebounder, but he was the leader of our team. Not to mention that he was one of my all-time favorite kids. He had a quiet unassuming nature about him ... no ego, or agenda, just a quiet kid that loved to play the game. I could not imagine any scenario that Calvin could be involved in something like this. I mean ... we were close! Beyond player and coach ... we had even been in Bible study together. "Are they sure it was Calvin? I asked. "Yes, Russell said. The detective wore a listening device, and they have the whole thing recorded."

I began the long, five-hour drive back to Shawnee, thinking and wondering how this could happen. Based on what Denna had told me; this appeared to be an open and shut case. They had caught Calvin red-handed... with both the audio recording, and a positive identification from the undercover police officer. My thoughts first turned selfish ... this would affect my credibility with the administration at OBU, would likely damage my reputation and career, and could derail our season by losing our best player. Not to mention the public relations nightmare that was anticipated and would obviously be coming soon. The media feeds on stuff like this ... a college sports star caught dealing drugs, even though we were a small private school. But then my thoughts turned to Calvin. Why would he do something like this? Would he go to prison? Would this ruin his life? By the time I got home to Shawnee, the OBU administrators were already meeting and strategizing. Their goal was to minimize the collateral damage from the media reports ... and do everything they could do to maintain their reputation and separate themselves from Calvin. OBU drew much of its support and student enrollment from its Southern Baptist constituency. The OBU niche was the fact that it was a small Baptist school, with a strong academic reputation. Sports and athletics were mostly a way to raise money and recruit students, and there were some on campus who looked upon the athletic department as nothing more than a necessary evil. The academic reputation was mostly a result of the school's own self-promotion and marketing, but a scandal in the basketball program was damaging to the entire university and its mission. There was no football here ... and men's basketball carried the torch for the entire athletic department. While I definitely cared about the reputation of our school, I was most concerned with Calvin, our basketball program, and of course, the effect this might have on my coaching career.

By the time I got to campus, word had already begun to leak

out, and some media outlets were reporting the incident, even with the limited information available to them. It was just a matter of time until the story came out and obviously, we would have to respond. The school's administration had already prepared a statement to release to the media. It was the usual paid political announcement ... "we won't comment on an ongoing police investigation ... we take pride in our school and in no way is this a reflection on our university or students ... we will not tolerate any illegal drug use or activity." I actually signed off on the statement because it had to be done, even if it was repetitive rhetoric that is just a slightly different version of the accepted norm in these kinds of situations. But in an effort to mitigate the media damage, OBU went a step further. Calvin Moore was not only suspended from all basketball-related activities, but he was also dismissed from the university, effective immediately. This seemed extremely premature to me ... partly because I knew Calvin better than anyone else on campus, and still believed in him, even if he had made this egregious error in judgment. I also knew that basketball was Calvin's only real shot in life. Maybe as a professional player, but at least to be used as a means to earn a college degree. Calvin had no real family life ... I never met his dad, and his mom was only peripherally involved in his life. He came from a tough home life and background, with no real emphasis on the value of a college education. But Calvin was far from being a dumb kid. He wasn't the most academically motivated, but he made his grades and easily maintained his academic eligibility. And he realized that basketball was his ticket to a better life. He loved the game, worked really hard at it, and was super coachable.

Eligibility rules for participation in intercollegiate athletics can sometimes be complicated. Many outsiders don't realize that as a student-athlete, you have only ten semesters to complete your four years of eligibility. And if you transfer from one school to another, rules require that you sit out a full year to establish residency. The rules have changed now and are dramatically different, but this was the generally accepted rule in 1989. Calvin had previously utilized a redshirt year, when he sat out and did not participate. So, in the fall semester of 1989, he was entering his ninth semester. This meant that the practical effect of his dismissal from OBU was that it ended his career as a player. He could not transfer to another school and be eligible to play, and he would not be permitted to remain in school at

OBU. Calvin was done. OBU thought they would be best served to completely cut ties with Calvin and disassociate the university completely from him. It was unfair to Calvin, not to mention the total absence of any due process. But to the university, he had been charged and was deemed guilty. While I had to publicly support the university's decision to sever its relationship with Calvin, I was privately angry at the rush to judgment at the expense of this young man's education, basketball career, and potential livelihood.

A few days after I arrived back on campus, the word came that Calvin had been assigned a court-appointed attorney, since he obviously had no resources to hire his own counsel. He was represented by Stephen Goforth, a young attorney who was still cutting his teeth in criminal law. Calvin made bail with financial help from his girlfriend, and he was released from county lockup. The first thing he did was come to see me.

Calvin walked into my office with his head down, obviously ashamed and embarrassed. We began to talk. He looked me in the eye and maintained his innocence, saying that this was a case of mistaken identity. The police were simply wrong, he told me. But he had no evidence or even a valid or persuasive argument for his innocence. He just said they were wrong. He pleaded with me to believe him, and I wanted to. But there was clear evidence, a tape recording and a positive ID from a most credible witness, the undercover cop that said he bought drugs from Calvin. I didn't see any way out of this. I told him I would speak with his attorney and would do everything I could do to help. Calvin left my office, and I immediately called Goforth to set up a meeting. I got the feeling from our phone conversation that Goforth really wanted to help, though he admitted that Calvin had little chance of surviving this prosecution. The evidence seemed to convincingly point to Calvin. Goforth had obtained a copy of the voice recording, and it seemed like a slam-dunk case for the prosecution. We agreed to meet ... and he'd let me listen to the recording and look at the police report. But the type, amount of drugs, and its street value ... would mean Calvin would likely go to prison. College coaches are ultimately held responsible for the behavior of their players ... so as much as I was worried about Calvin, I was equally concerned about my job, as well as our team. I arranged a meeting with Goforth for the next day.

When Goforth came to my office the next morning we quickly got to the point. I read the police report which was quite detailed and compelling. I asked about possible defenses for Calvin ... Calvin was African American; was there a chance it was a result of racial profiling? Goforth said that would be a stretch since the arresting officer was also black. He thought the best course of action was to try and reach a plea agreement with the district attorney. But to do that, Calvin would obviously have to admit his guilt and would probably still do time in the penitentiary. Calvin continued to maintain his innocence, to both me and his attorney. Goforth asked me to talk with Calvin again and discuss with him the benefits of a plea deal. I agreed to do so. As he stood up to leave, I asked him if I could listen to the tape from the police detective. I got the recorder out and he gave me the cassette tape. I had agreed with Goforth that the best plan of action was likely the pursuit of a plea deal, with all the evidence mounted against his client. But after listening to the tape, it became evident that there was a big problem for the district attorney...because the voice on the recording WAS NOT CALVIN MOORE!

"The grass withers and the flowers fall, but the word of our God stands forever." Isaiah 40:8

CHAPTER 2 – BEYOND THE SCOREBOARD

The police had it all wrong! After listening to the recording, I was astonished that the voice was not that of Calvin Moore. I told Goforth that the voice on the tape wasn't Calvin's, and my claim was met with immediate skepticism. Goforth thought maybe I was trying to save my player and salvage his eligibility for basketball. But with his dismissal from school, that was not possible. First, I had to convince Goforth that I had no selfish motive. We had just met each other for the first time, and he had no way of knowing if I could be trusted. He asked if I would be willing to testify in court that the voice was not Calvin. I sure did not want to do that and asked him about getting a professional voice analysis. But he explained that it was likely cost prohibitive and that the science of voice analysis was still considered suspect. He said if I was sure that it was not Calvin on the tape, I would need to testify, even if we decided to go with an outside voice analysis. He pressed me several times about how sure I was… how could I know 100%, and did I have any motivations for not telling the truth? Goforth and everyone else at the university had just assumed that Calvin was guilty. This was an open-and-shut case … how could the detectives get it wrong? They had a police officer eyewitness, a positive identification from a trained undercover officer, and it was all recorded on tape. I wanted to believe Calvin when he said he was innocent … but even I had my doubts until I heard the tape. He offered no evidence or even an explanation of how he had become the accused. But I was positive that it was not Calvin's voice on that recording. So, I had been truthful with Goforth and was reluctantly willing to testify to prove the innocence of my now ex-best player. He thanked me and left my office saying he would be in touch. I wasn't sure Goforth actually believed me, but it was his job to represent his client as best he could, and my testimony would be an absolute bombshell for the defense. But I was holding out on Calvin's attorney by a secret that I failed to tell him. The reason I knew it wasn't Calvin on the recording was because I recognized the voice. It was one of my other players, Jace Evans.

Evans was one of our better players, and like Calvin, was a

transfer student. The two had actually become good friends. Evans was an athletic type that played over the rim. He and Calvin were an almost unstoppable tandem, with versatility to play more than one position. Jace was a likable more outgoing version of Calvin that brought his best efforts every day. And though I had been concerned about how these guys would fit into our culture at OBU, the truth is that they had assimilated very well. Most had embraced the Christian tone of our school and had done surprisingly well on the academic side. Our team GPA and graduation rate would not be anything worth bragging about, but they were progressing towards a degree. This recruiting class, and specifically Calvin and the other MCC players, more than anyone, helped to change the losing culture of our basketball program. These were the players that were mostly responsible for turning it around. They were meeting and exceeding my expectations on and off the court, and I genuinely liked these guys.

But now I am faced with this. Our best player had been dismissed from school, and one of our other players was apparently selling cocaine on the streets of Shawnee, Oklahoma. Our basketball program was coming apart at the seams, and I was facing the ultimate moral dilemma.

Calvin and Jace both came from lower socioeconomic environments, and both saw basketball as their ticket to a better life. This was not uncommon, especially back in the '80s, even more so than today. Calvin was awaiting trial, but his playing career was over. If I told university officials what I knew, Jace's playing days would end as well. But could I, in good conscience, play another season with one of our best players as an apparent drug dealer? I decided that I should first talk to Goforth and level with him.

The next week I called the attorney to see if he had any information about a voice analysis expert. He said he had checked around, but that it had only confirmed what he previously thought. It would be very expensive, and the testimony would be challenged since there's so much uncertainty about the science behind it. The prosecution would be able to poke holes in that testimony, citing numerous examples of this sort of analysis that ended up being incorrect. He was basically saying that Calvin's fate would largely be determined by the persuasiveness of my testimony.

It was then that I went full disclosure with Goforth. I had recognized the voice on the recording and knew the identity of the guilty party as Jace Evans, one of our other players.

I wanted to make it clear that I didn't want this to get out publicly. I had already lost my best player and couldn't afford to lose another. Calvin's playing career was over, and there was nothing fair about it. He didn't do this. Basketball is his life and now that's gone for him. The last thing I want to do is end the career of another player. It's all he has… and it might be his only chance at a better life. Goforth pledged to keep Evans' identity confidential. But he warned me that I might have to identify the guilty party in order to help Calvin get cleared of this charge. He understood my concern about the other player but said the most important thing to consider is that we make certain an innocent young man does not go to prison. I agreed but asked the attorney to find a way to do this without implicating my other player. Then I gave him the speech. "I wanna be clear. I don't condone the use or sale of illegal street drugs. There's no excuse for it and I'll be the last one to try and excuse one of my players if he's guilty. But so many of these players have no means of support. I know the backgrounds they come from. They're on a full scholarship here, but that hardly covers all their expenses. They don't have family financial support and collegiate rules prohibit them from working while on an athletic scholarship. So, it's enticing if a kid sees a way to make some easy money, in order to support themselves. It doesn't make it right, but I do understand the temptation. I just don't see how ruining another kid's life is the direction we need to go." Maybe that was how I really felt … or maybe I was just trying to justify my decision to keep Jace out of this. But either way, Goforth said he agreed and assured me that he would do his best to keep Jace's exposure to a minimum.

I thanked him again for his help and remember wondering if he really agreed with me. I'm not even sure that we were doing the right thing. Was I motivated to try to save a kid's life, or just selfishly trying to save my season and career? Still unsure of the answer but looking back at it years later I can guess it was probably both. So, the decision was made as to my course of action. I would absolutely try to keep Calvin out of prison … he was after all, innocent of these charges. But I also decided to keep the identity of the voice confidential. No one on campus knew the truth about Jace, and most were still convinced that Calvin was guilty as charged.

I was still the coach at OBU, and I had an upcoming season to play. I directed my efforts toward getting the team ready to play the season. With Calvin, there was so much reason for optimism, and the community was genuinely excited about the upcoming season. We had been ranked nationally in the preseason polls and considered the favorite to win our league. But without our best player from last year, our championship hopes were significantly dimmed.

Calvin was out on bail and staying with his girlfriend in Shawnee. He could not leave the jurisdiction and was not allowed on campus by the OBU administration, which had to be difficult. His friends were here, and he could not even come and watch a practice or a game. The team was getting ready for the season, but I kept in touch with Goforth every week.

Expectations for the season were tempered by the absence of Calvin. But my job was to help the squad move forward without him and be the best we could be. We had good players, experienced and cohesive. I didn't know how good we could be, but to everyone's surprise, we started the season with nine straight wins. Willie Gilmore, also from MCC, was terrific and seemed destined for all-conference honors. Our other guys rallied and played with confidence. When the first poll came out in January, there we were... ranked #1 in the nation ... a first in OBU history. The community and students were excited, and we were playing in front of a packed house on most nights.

I hadn't talked with Calvin recently ... Goforth thought it best if I had no contact since I'd be testifying at trial. But his court date was approaching, and I had one final meeting with Goforth to discuss strategy. The game plan was simple ... and I was Calvin's only witness and only defense. The prosecution would put on its case, and then I would take the stand for the defense. It would be a one-day trial according to Goforth since there would likely only be two witnesses. The prosecution would put on the undercover detective who recorded the illegal drug sale, and then I would be called to the stand to testify. Goforth's plan was to ask me only a few key questions.

Was this Calvin Moore on the recording? Did I have any reason or motivation to not be truthful? Could I be sure that the voice was not that of Jace Evans?

I took issue with the last question because I thought it subtly pointed the finger at Evans.

But Goforth was adamant that we could not exclude the voice on the tape from being one of my other players, and this would allow the jury to know that we weren't trying to falsely protect anyone. This is a way to NOT identify the voice as that of Jace he said but rather strengthen your statement that it's not Calvin. I reluctantly agreed to answer all the questions before me, hoping Calvin could get cleared of the charges without any more collateral damage to anyone else on our team. It's understandable that others might take issue with the decision not to be totally forthcoming about Jace's involvement. And I'll admit it's certainly not my finest hour as a college basketball coach. But it seemed the right thing to do at the time, and years later looking back, I'd probably arrive at the same conclusion later in my career. I was doing what I could to help Calvin stay out of prison with a wrongful conviction without hurting another player. Calvin's basketball career was over, that much was certain. There was no going back after OBU had dismissed him from school. He was out of time and out of eligibility. And even if that had not been the case, other schools were not likely to take a player who had been accused of selling cocaine. There was nothing more to do now but wait for the trial.

In the meantime, the team had dropped a couple of games, but we were still mostly winning. We were in first place in our conference and remained nationally ranked. I learned that Calvin's trial was scheduled the day before our game at Northeastern Oklahoma, against my former college coach at Tulsa, Ken Hayes. I did my best to prepare our team for the game, but my mind was mostly on Calvin.

I reported to the courthouse the morning of the trial, nervous as any witness would be. The lawyers made a brief opening statement, then the prosecution put the arresting officer on the stand. His testimony was that Calvin had sold him a large amount of cocaine while he was working undercover. The district attorney played the audio tape and then asked the detective to point out the person in the courtroom who sold him the illegal drugs. He pointed directly at Calvin. It was the only witness for the prosecution, and I'd be up next. Goforth started by asking some basic background information. He hammered home the point that I had no motive to give false or misleading testimony. Then it came time to ask the deciding question of the trial … "Was this the voice of Calvin Moore on the recording?" I answered truthfully that it wasn't Calvin, but that I couldn't be sure it wasn't another player on my team. I also gave the jury a short version of the rules governing collegiate basketball that prevented Calvin from ever playing in college again. From a straight basketball perspective, Calvin had absolutely nothing to gain from my testimony. But it was my testimony and mine only, that had the potential to keep Calvin Moore from going to prison.

Now I don't know if the district attorney was surprised by my testimony or not. But he sure looked like it. The judge asked if he wanted to cross-examine. He did not.

Both lawyers rested their case and made some brief closing statements. The entire trial had only lasted a few hours and was now in the hands of the jury.

I left the courthouse and went back to campus to have our final practice before our road game at Northeastern. Goforth said it wasn't likely the jury would have a verdict on the same day as the trial but that it should conclude tomorrow. It's not like they had a lot of information or testimony to go over. It basically came down to the detective's eyewitness account and positive ID, against my testimony that refuted the testimony of the police. The next day we got word that the jury was back with a decision. We were on the road at Northeastern so I could not be there for Calvin. But our radio announcer, John Parrish, had an open phone line and was keeping tabs on what was happening back in Shawnee. We would know the outcome shortly after it was announced in the courtroom. We were in the gym at Northeastern, going through our normal shoot-around and walk-through a few hours before tipoff. Out of the corner of my eye, I saw Parrish walking briskly towards me. He was smiling. Then he blurted it out … IT'S NOT GUILTY! Win and I had our own quiet little celebration. We didn't want to distract the players. This was a big game for us, and they needed to stay focused. The players would know the outcome soon.

We defeated Northeastern that night and went on to win a conference championship that year. We lost in the finals of our district tournament which ended our season at 27-5.

Losing in the district finals kept us out of the national tournament in Kansas City because there were no at-large berths back in those days. It was win or go home. But we were conference champions, had completed our third straight winning season, and recorded the most wins in school history. I was voted the league's coach of the year for the second straight season, and Willie Gilmore won player of the year honors. It had been a successful season, albeit with a bittersweet ending.

Calvin Moore, having been wrongfully charged walked out of the courtroom as a free man. But he never played another day of organized basketball. His career was over, having been dismissed from the university that was just trying to protect its image by distancing itself from an accused student. OBU reaped the rewards of a championship season, and I got a new contract extension. I didn't know it at the time, but I would never coach another game at Oklahoma Baptist University. And I never saw Calvin Moore again.

"May He give you the desire of your heart and make all your plans succeed." Psalms 20:4

CHAPTER 3 - THE NEW CHIEF

With a conference championship, three straight winning seasons, and a new contract at OBU I felt relieved. Some of the pressure to win had subsided. But out of nowhere came a new opportunity in my coaching career. Legendary coach Abe Lemons was retiring as head coach of the Oklahoma City University Chiefs. Abe was a legend and a celebrity in Oklahoma, on the same level as the state's favorite son and humorist, Will Rogers. He had just completed his second stint at OCU after leaving the first time to become the head coach at Texas-Pan American and then at the University of Texas. His 1978 team at Texas won the NIT Championship and he also led the UT program to two conference championships. The program at Oklahoma City had gone through tons of recent changes. Its tradition was mostly launched at the Division One level of basketball, but it was now a member of the NAIA. Its storied past was based mostly on the success of one man, Coach Abe Lemons. Oklahoma City boasted the first major college holiday basketball tournament in the country that began back in the 1930's. The All-College Tournament, as it was called, attracted some of the best college teams in the country as well as some of the best players ever to play the game. I remember practically living at the State Fairgrounds arena in Oklahoma City during the three-day tourney, watching the likes of Pete Maravich, Calvin Murphy, Artis Gilmore and other greats. OCU was a mainstay in the tournament, and the players were like royalty to the basketball fans in the city … and especially to kids with big dreams. This was way before games were televised, and it was a treat to see players that we could otherwise only read about. The games were always a tough ticket to get hold of and sellout crowds were commonplace. OCU always seemed to have good success in the tournament, with a definite home-court advantage even though the games were played away from campus at the Fairgrounds Arena. The All-College tournament continued until 2016 before the tournament market became saturated by sponsorship from the sneaker companies and ESPN events.

Abe Lemons was a sought-after speaker on the Nike circuit and despite being a legitimately great basketball coach, he was always good for a few laughs and was highly entertaining. He was just a small-town kid from Walters, Oklahoma and brought unprecedented notoriety to this small school that was competing against the biggest and most successful programs in the nation. It was 1989 when Abe announced that this would be his last season at OCU, and it was time to retire. My mentor at Oklahoma State University, Paul Hansen, had been Abe's long-time assistant at OCU, before taking over the reins as head coach when Abe left for Pan American. Paul had great success in his own right at OCU and soon left to become the head man at Oklahoma State. So, when Abe retired, I ended up with the two most influential OCU coaches in school history recommending me for the job that Abe had just vacated. With these two heavyweights backing me, I was a shoo-in to land the head coaching gig at Oklahoma City University. Even though it was now in the same league as Oklahoma Baptist, it was clearly a better job. The compensation level was higher, it was easier to recruit to Oklahoma City, it had a tradition at the division one level, and I had the endorsement from two Oklahoma coaching legends. Becoming the head coach at Oklahoma City University was not just a new start in my career. But it was also sort of a childhood dream come true. For a kid who grew up in suburban Oklahoma City, I was well aware of the proud tradition of the OCU Chiefs. I walked into OCU as its head coach following a living legend, who had almost single-handedly kept this school afloat through its success on the basketball court. These were some big shoes to fill indeed.

Big-time college basketball, and college sports in general, is full of hypocrisy. We're expected to win games at a high level while educating these players, with above-average graduation rates, all the while doing our best to help create solid citizens for society. It's a noble cause, but the rhetoric about the educational part can sometimes be a bit more about style than substance. The truth is that fans and supporters want a winning program and all that goes with it. Winning programs bring money into the university while getting the kind of publicity that you can't buy. Enrollment numbers are often correlated with how well your sports programs are doing. I had felt somewhat duped at my previous school, Oklahoma Baptist University. The mandate I had been given at OBU was to bring in quality students, interested primarily in education. There wasn't much discussion about any pressure to win... mediocrity was acceptable as long as our program aligned itself with the same values, goals, and philosophies that were consistent with the university as a whole. I wanted to win and felt I could do it in the manner that the OBU brass wanted. The administration made it clear that taking junior college transfers or short-term student/athletes with little chance to graduate would be frowned upon, if not impermissible. So, we recruited mostly Oklahoma high school kids who would represent the university in a positive manner while succeeding academically. What resulted was a bunch of great kids who were academically minded but weren't talented enough to win games at a high level. Our team GPA went through the roof, but we were losing games badly. And the tone of the administration shifted dramatically when we had back-to-back losing seasons. Now all of a sudden, we needed to WIN! And we did win eventually. But now at OCU, I was at a place that wanted to compete at a high level and had clear aspirations of winning a national championship and was not apologizing for it.

OCU President Dr. Jerald Walker was impressed by our turnaround at OBU, and with Lemons and Hansen on board, he was strongly in my corner. Walker gave us everything we needed to be successful. Our budget was good, we had more scholarships than most other small college programs, and the most important thing ... he let me bring in the assistant coach I needed. Win Case, who I had recruited to Oklahoma State and then hired at OBU was my guy. He was the best recruiter I had ever been around, he had a charming personality, a keen basketball IQ, and was a proven winner. Win was the best assistant I ever had, and the individual that I felt could help us get to that championship level that Dr. Walker wanted. We were beyond excited about the new job and about being together again. But now it was time to get to work. Abe had left us a good team, but we had some holes to fill. Filling out our roster with quality players was our top priority and we hit the ground running. We had solid players already and we knew we were good enough to compete, but not good enough to win championships. We needed a star player to take us to the next level. But we had no idea where our first recruiting class at OCU would take us. We also had no idea that we were about to make college basketball history.

"We can make our plans, but it is the Lord that determines our steps." Proverbs 16:9

CHAPTER 4 - ODD MAN OUT

I met Denna when I was an assistant coach at Oklahoma State University. I was one of the youngest major college assistants in the country and she was a graduating senior at OSU. We had both been thrown together by my old college roommate at the University of Tulsa who now, coincidentally, lived next door to Denna's family in Tulsa. He was encouraging both of us to meet until finally one day at his urging, Denna showed up at our practice facility in Gallagher Hall on the OSU campus. We met and talked briefly at the arena, and I followed up with a phone call later that night. My coaching career was at the absolute center stage of my life but as I look back, Denna was the first girl to ever take my attention off of basketball, at least for the moment. She was tall, smart, virtuous, and stunningly beautiful. We began dating but she had plans for graduate school out of state once she completed her undergraduate degree in geology. But I was a recruiter now and she was a blue chipper. It was almost immediately that I felt certain this was the girl I would marry. I put on the full-court press and in two months we were engaged. I remember honestly thinking to myself that I needed to close this deal before I had a chance to mess things up because she was clearly out of my league. We got married a week after her graduation in May of 1985, and after I had just accepted my first college head coaching job at Oklahoma Baptist University. She gave up the idea of graduate school to begin the journey with me. Denna took an entry-level geology job in Oklahoma City, about 45 minutes from OBU. It was the beginning of what turned out to be an illustrious career in her field, but for now she mostly just settled in her new role as a coach's wife. Being the wife of a coach is a huge adjustment for anyone. It has the ups and downs of a roller coaster and of course, it's a very public life you lead. Every coach is the subject of intense scrutiny by those who are mostly unqualified to critique the job you're doing. Fans, students, supporters, and alumni can often be brutal, especially in the midst of a losing season. The coach's spouse must endure the criticism with a thick skin and stay loyal to the one person she loves more than anyone else. Denna was the ultimate coach's wife. She was supportive throughout all the good and bad times and never wavered in her loyalty to me and my career ambitions. And while I appreciated her and loved her dearly, she very often took a back seat to the job and career aspirations that were all-encompassing. My job had become my life, and it was like having a mistress. It consumed my days and nights as well as my thoughts. I was determined to win games, advance my career, climb the ladder, and ultimately win championships. Everything else in life had become incidental, including my marriage. But Denna had a Godly faith that sustained her through a marriage that had become strained, and a husband that was living in the limelight of selfish ambition. But she never complained, and she never stopped supporting my dreams.

I had made a profession of my faith in Jesus Christ when I was in high school at the age of fifteen. I followed up with baptism, joined the church, prayed every day, attended church camps and felt relieved to be saved by the grace of God. I was confident that Jesus was my lord and savior, but I can't really say that my decision to follow Christ had changed my life. It carried me through some tough times in high school and college, and early in my coaching career. But mostly I was a casual Christian, attending church irregularly and taking only a passing interest in my own spiritual growth. I had led a team Bible study at OBU, but it was more out of a sense of duty and to satisfy an administration that I considered at the time to be little more than religious zealots. So truthfully, I went through the motions of living out my faith, mostly to advance the career that I was so passionate about. My marriage to Denna had suffered because we were less than equally yoked in our faith, and my life's priorities had taken an unhealthy turn. But she hung in there, always supportive, and always giving. The year was 1990 and it was a monumental one for us. I resigned as coach at OBU and accepted the job as head coach of the Oklahoma City University Chiefs. It was the same year that Denna and I welcomed a newborn son into the world, Derek Paul Johnson. Life was good.

Dr. Bob Agee, President at OBU tried to talk me out of going to OCU. He even suggested that Gerald Walker, OCU President, had unrealistic expectations and would be hard to work for. He talked about how much I had grown as a coach over the years and even took credit for giving me enough time to turn the program around. But in truth, I was the same coach I had always been. We turned the program into a winner by recruiting better athletes and improving our roster each year. We had taken some second-chance type players and some others who were academically suspect. They were mostly good kids but hardly fit the stereotype of the average OBU student profile. But we won ... and despite the mandate I had been given at the beginning of my tenure at the school about recruiting academically motivated players that could graduate, the winning seemed to satisfy the OBU administration. I could not forget how close I was to losing my job at OBU, which would likely have ended my career. I was somewhat bitter about what I perceived as the hypocrisy of OBU leadership. So, there were no second thoughts about leaving for OCU. It was a fresh start with university leadership that was clear about what was expected of us. Here are the tools ... now go win championships.

    The transition to OCU was a joy ride. We were on our honeymoon as a new coaching staff with abundant hopes and dreams. For a coach, the best time of the year is the off-season and preseason. Your team hasn't suffered a loss yet, and there's always a reason for optimism. It might just be the proverbial "we'll get 'em next year" but in college basketball, you're never more than a couple of key players away from getting things turned around. We had a team of solid role players going into our first year at OCU. But we lacked star power and the expectation for the Chiefs was to win now. We weren't really interested in taking young and unproven players. We needed guys that were ready now to take this to a championship level. That meant we were locking in on junior college and division one transfers. And in 1990, there was one prize recruit in the entire country that stood out among all the rest. He was a game changer, a certain all-American with a big-time pedigree. His name was Eric Manuel.

    Eric had been a high school Parade and McDonalds All-American at Macon (Ga) Southwest High School and was considered one of the top five players in the country after his senior year in 1987. After graduating from high school, he became the prize recruit for Coach Eddie Sutton's Kentucky Wildcat squad. Eric became an instant starter at Kentucky and was named to the All-SEC freshman team in 1988. But there was an ongoing NCAA investigation into Eric's eligibility at Kentucky, and a dark cloud hovering over his future with the Wildcats. Allegations of academic fraud surfaced when Eric's ACT score took a nine-point jump in his second attempt to qualify for NCAA eligibility. The NCAA also called into question the circumstances surrounding the test itself. It seemed that Coach Sutton's son, Sean, had driven Eric to the testing site, and took the test at the same time as Manuel. Eric sat out the 1988-89 season at Kentucky while the NCAA in typical fashion took its time investigating the matter. The NCAA finally finished its investigation in 1989 and determined that Eric, or someone associated with the Kentucky program, had falsified ACT test answers. The Manuel case came to light when the NCAA was investigating Kentucky for an entirely different matter. In what was later termed the "Bills and Mills" affair, the NCAA found that assistant coach Dwayne Casey had sent cash through express mail to Kentucky recruit Chris Mills. Casey and Sutton both resigned from their coaching positions, and Sean Sutton was charged with lying to NCAA investigators. Eric was said to have likely cheated on his second ACT test, an allegation that Eric Manuel still denies to this day. But the NCAA was basing its decision on the mathematical improbability that Manuel could have legitimately raised his test score to this degree. The principals in the scandal at Kentucky had very different outcomes. Eddie Sutton emerged as the new head coach at Oklahoma State University, his alma mater. Dwayne Casey eventually landed in the NBA, holding head coaching positions with the Toronto Raptors, the Minnesota Timberwolves, and the Detroit Pistons. He also settled a multi-million-dollar lawsuit against Emory packaging, after large sums of cash were discovered being sent from Casey to Chris Mills. Sean Sutton had his charges dropped by the NCAA and played for his father at Oklahoma State, eventually becoming the head coach there. Chris Mills played Division One basketball and went on to play professionally in the NBA. Eric Manuel, on the other hand, was banned for life from ever playing at another NCAA institution. It seems the NCAA wanted to make an example out of Manuel, giving him what is thought to be the only lifetime ban the NCAA has ever imposed on a student athlete. While it's likely that irregularities on Eric's second test did in fact occur, it's also entirely plausible that Eric was completely innocent of any wrongdoing. With no option of Eric ever competing at an NCAA program, he enrolled at Hiwassee Junior College in Tennessee to continue playing and working towards a college degree. This was a far cry from major college basketball, especially at a place like Kentucky which routinely attracts NBA-caliber talent. But junior college was Eric's only possibility of continuing in college basketball. He not only loved basketball, but he excelled in every aspect of the game and desperately wanted to play in college. So, the 1988-89 basketball season saw Eric playing for Hiwassee and earning All-American status for his play on the court. More importantly, Eric made good grades, was an exemplary student, and graduated with an associate's degree. Under NCAA rules, even if Eric had been a non-qualifier out of high school, he would now certainly be eligible to play at an NCAA institution because of his grades and successful graduation. But there was still the issue of the lifetime ban the NCAA had handed down. The NCAA enforcement staff and infractions committee had actually overruled and broken its own set of regulations in this case. Eric was eligible to play by NCAA rules by meeting all the degree requirements at Hiwassee but was still prevented from furthering his college playing career at an NCAA school. His choices now were to turn pro and make himself available for the NBA draft or maybe play overseas. Or would he possibly have any interest in playing for an NAIA school since they had no affiliation with the NCAA? It was definitely worth looking into and my first step would be to lay it all out with the OCU administration. I scheduled an appointment with President Walker and OCU athletic director, Bud Sahmaunt.

    I went into the meeting having done my homework. We discovered that most of the heavyweight NAIA schools were already recruiting Eric. And we had also learned that by all accounts, this was an outstanding young man, on and off the basketball court. Our intel was solid, that cheating on an exam would be out of character for Eric Manuel, and that his intangibles (work ethic, attitude, dedication, etc.) were off the chart. But I knew that if we signed Eric there would be some backlash, and possibly some negative publicity. Eric's story and the Kentucky scandal had become highly publicized. Sports Illustrated ran a feature story about Manuel in its February 1991 issue, entitled "Odd Man Out." Everyone with any interest in college basketball knew about Eric's story. Many administrators would shy away from recruiting a student-athlete with such a checkered past and with the academic cloud surrounding his NCAA eligibility. But the primary question Dr. Walker asked in our meeting was "Can we get him?" Of course, there was no certain answer to that question, but I definitely wanted to try. Walker was sold and gave us the go-ahead. The decision to try and recruit Eric to OCU was huge and indicative of the type of college President we had at the school. Walker wanted to win, and he wasn't against giving a kid a chance, even one with a very negative public image that had been portrayed by every major media outlet in the country. The Kentucky scandal had landed the basketball program on NCAA probation and had cost coaches their jobs. But it could be argued that the penalty levied against Eric was the most costly of all. The NCAA had taken away a kid's dream, and it was based on compelling but circumstantial evidence at best. We began the process of trying to make Eric Manuel an OCU Chief. We knew this would be a highly competitive recruitment, and we weren't even sure if Eric would entertain the idea of playing small college basketball after having a taste of the big time at the University of Kentucky. But we decided to go full tilt in the recruitment of Eric, knowing that he was the caliber of player that could single-handedly vault our program to a championship level. I thanked Dr. Walker for his decision that allowed us the opportunity to recruit Eric. And I'll never forget his response as we began to leave the meeting ... "I believe in giving our new coach enough rope to hang himself with." He was smiling when he said it but with a serious, business-like tone in his voice. But that did not deter us even for a moment. Just the idea of having such a player on our team was exciting and might be a once-in-a-lifetime opportunity. It was definitely a long shot, but one we were willing to take. We had no idea the obstacles we would need to overcome to actually get Eric Manuel into an OCU uniform.

"Run in such a way to win the prize." 1 Corinthians 1:24

CHAPTER 5 - THE PURSUIT OF A SUPERSTAR

Eric Manuel hailed from the projects on the south side of Macon, Georgia. Throughout my career, I was repeatedly amazed at the number of quality kids who came from tough, sometimes impoverished, and often single-parent home environments. And I was equally surprised at some of the kids from privileged backgrounds who turned out to be high-maintenance types who lacked a high-level work ethic. There's nothing scientific about the generalization, but it sure has been my experience. Eric lived in public housing with his mom, Mary, and three brothers. Mary worked two, and sometimes three jobs, to support her boys as a single mom. Eric went to school, played basketball, and also held a part-time job at McDonalds to help out at home. The comedic irony cannot be lost that he was actually a first-team McDonalds All-American in high school, which is the most prestigious of any of the high school all-star awards. Still today, the McDonalds All-Star Game is one of the few high school events that is NBA-sanctioned and is considered a "must attend" for NBA scouts and front office personnel. Eric was a product of Southwest High School in Macon and coach "Duck" Williamson, who was a legendary coach in high school basketball circles. Duck had coached NBA stars Norm Nixon and Jeff Malone at Southwest and was no stranger to the throngs of college coaches who came knocking, seeking the services of his latest star, Eric Manuel. Eric had been recruited at Southwest by every high major program in the country before signing with Kentucky.

One of the tasks we had now, before recruiting Eric for OCU, was to somehow ingratiate ourselves with Eric's inner circle, including his high school coach, and of course his family. We had no real connections with Eric or his people, so we were working almost immediately from a disadvantage. We had a peripheral connection through Eddie Sutton, who had played and now coached at Oklahoma State. The Kentucky scandal was still fresh enough to Coach Sutton that it was clear that the last thing he wanted was a lingering connection with Eric Manuel. There would be a perception of "guilt by association" and Eddie wanted no part of Eric's recruitment, even residually. So, he was helpful enough when we contacted him, and it became obvious that he had a genuine affection for Eric himself. Eddie helped us get the lay of the land, as did some others, and eventually, we gathered enough information to at least make contact with Eric and his mom. So, we started calling. The point man on Eric's recruitment was my assistant coach, Win Case, who I still consider to be one of the best in the business. Win was a relentless recruiter, and he knew how valuable this prize recruit could be for our program, for the university as a whole, but also for our coaching careers. Win had played an instrumental part in the turnaround at OBU, recruiting most of the guys who ended up being the difference makers that produced three straight winning seasons and a #1 national ranking. If there was anyone that could make this happen with Eric, I felt it was Win Case.

Unlike the NCAA, NAIA rules are less cumbersome when it comes to recruiting. The premise behind much of the NAIA's rule book on recruiting is the desire for each member school to self-govern and act responsibly. So, we didn't have limits on phone calls or other contacts, except for budgetary constraints. We were prepared to spend our entire recruiting budget on Eric Manuel. Win started getting in touch with Eric and his inner circle. He was making inroads and spent most of his time trying to determine who the real decision-maker was going to be. In college recruiting, there's always someone close to the player that he trusts, that will end up influencing the decision of where he ends up going to school. But this case was different because Eric might not even go to school. He was by no means NBA-ready, but he might be able to make a comfortable living playing overseas. It would obviously be a major step down in the level of competition from Kentucky to OCU. But Win kept plugging away. He called Eric every day, sent notes to Mary, and flowers on her birthday. He was building a relationship and trust with Eric and his family. The motivation behind the building of the relationship is somewhat looked upon as selfish and one-sided. And certainly, there is some truth to that thought. But what made Win an effective recruiter was that he genuinely cared about these kids. We wanted to assemble a championship-level roster, but Win never lost sight of the human element. I learned a lot from him, especially about a genuine love and affection for the kids you coach. I maintain relationships with former players even today, and that is a monumental treasure to me. I've always maintained that you can coach kids as hard as you need to, as long as they know you have their best interests at heart, and that you truly care about their life in and out of basketball. We were making progress with Eric, to the point that he and Mary agreed to meet us at their home in Macon. This was a gigantic step in the recruiting process, to have an opportunity to sit down face to face with Eric and his mom. Shortly after the home visit invitation, Win and I boarded a plane from Oklahoma City to Atlanta. We were going to visit Eric Manuel.

Everyone thinks they can recruit. But it's a combination of art and science. When I made the jump from coaching at a small-town high school to a major college assistant, I thought I knew how to recruit, or that I could easily learn the ropes. My first year as an assistant at Oklahoma State was the same year the University of San Francisco dropped their men's basketball program. They had been plagued with NCAA violations, investigations, and allegations of off-court improprieties. Players at USF received a waiver from the NCAA to transfer without having to sit out a year to re-establish their eligibility. This was back before current NCAA rules which allow student-athletes to transfer with no penalty or residency requirement. So, when USF dismantled its program, this was an opportunity to poach experienced and proven players with remaining eligibility. USF had a 7'2 center named Rogue Harris, who would become my first attempt at college recruiting. I contacted Rogue about the possibility of transferring to Oklahoma State, and he ultimately committed to a campus visit to Stillwater, Oklahoma. This was way before the days of the internet, cell phones, and other technology so we relied on newspapers and word of mouth. So, we really didn't know much about Rogue, except for his college stats at USF and the fact that he was a seven-footer. We sent a plane to Oklahoma City to pick up Rogue and bring him to Stillwater after his commercial flight from San Francisco. So, in the summer of 1982, Rogue Harris steps off the plane in Stillwater with hair down to his waist tied back in a ponytail, multiple piercings, and a tattoo on his shoulder that read "This Bud's for You." My boss and head coach Paul Hansen looked at me and said, "You're doing a heckuva job!" As it turned out, Rogue was way ahead of his time and was a non-fit for Stillwater, Oklahoma in 1982. He signed with the University of Hawaii and had a mediocre college career. Clearly, I had a long way to go, and a lot to learn about recruiting at this level.

But now we were on our way to see Eric Manuel, the best player Win and I had ever recruited. We were more seasoned now, highly motivated, and excited to the point of giddiness about the possibility of bringing Eric to OCU. We rented a car at the Atlanta airport and made the two-hour drive to Macon. We had directions to the public housing development where Mary and her boys lived, knowing what was at stake with the upcoming visit. Both of us had done this plenty of times, but this would be different. We had spoken on the phone with Mary and Eric numerous times, but this was our first time in person. Mary Manuel was a most gracious hostess, and Eric was mostly quiet during the visit. We couldn't read him very well but became convinced that his mom was the most influential person in Eric's life and would have the biggest voice in the decision. As we talked and listened, it became clear that Mary wanted Eric to go to school and continue working towards his four-year degree. This was the first major hurdle. Eric was going to school to play basketball and to complete his undergraduate education. The NCAA had dug in their heels and remained adamant that the lifetime ban for Eric Manuel would remain in effect, and that there was no appealing that decision. So, the only option remaining for Eric was to attend a non-NCAA institution, and likely an NAIA school. Mary was confident in her son's abilities on the court, so we mostly talked about the importance of his education. OCU had, and still has, a reputation for academic excellence. Mary asked a lot of questions about graduation rates, tutors for student-athletes, study table, and our commitment to our players getting their degrees. We were ready with the answers and went into detail about our personalized educational plan for Eric. She seemed to like us, and we felt good about the approximate two-hour conversation. But the most important thing we got out of the meeting was a commitment from Eric and Mary to take an official visit to our campus. We wanted Eric to meet our players, staff, faculty, and other students ... and to see for himself what life at OCU was really like. We left the meeting feeling optimistic, and that our primary mission had been accomplished. We established some chemistry with Eric and Mary and got the official visit commitment. We also got an encouraging sign from Eric as we were leaving his home after dark in the projects of Macon, Georgia. It was then that he said, "Coach, you better let me walk you to your car," obviously concerned about our personal safety.

It was full speed ahead with his recruitment. Eric had made visits to other NAIA campuses, but I've always said that OCU was the best non-division job in the country. We had tradition, a great city, a strong fan base, and with Eric, we could have the makings of a championship team. We spent weeks planning Eric's visit to campus with no stone left unturned. Summer was upon us by now, which was late in the recruiting process, so we felt like we had a real chance to sign Eric. His visit was planned out to the finest detail. While Mary's point of emphasis was on her son's education, Eric seemed more interested in where he would live, what the food was like, and oh yeah ... where are the girls?

From our standpoint, the visit couldn't have gone any better. We put our absolute best foot forward and everyone stepped up. It's critical for current players to be involved when prospects visit campus. Recruits want to know the guys they'll be spending most of their time with. But it's a delicate situation with current players when recruits visit. Sometimes players feel threatened by the prospects, especially when they play the same position. I've actually had players try and sabotage a recruit's visit because they were insecure about playing time or their position on the team. We always tell our players that competition for positions makes everyone better and ultimately makes our team better. That's why it's so important to recruit players that will thrive in a team-oriented structure and want to put team goals ahead of their own. It's walking a fine line for sure. But we had everyone on board with Eric's visit. They seemed to know that he could elevate this team to a championship contender, which is what everyone wanted. The guys did great with Eric on the visit and made him feel at home. This was crucial. The kid had been through so much already and had been dragged through the media mud. He just wanted to be a regular guy and play the game he loved. On Eric's last day of his visit he verbally committed to attend OCU and to becoming a part of our program. Everything seemed to be a perfect fit for him ... basketball-wise, socially, and educationally. He was genuinely excited about becoming an OCU Chief.

Verbal commitments are non-binding of course, and we didn't want to take anything for granted. We were only a few weeks away from the start of the Fall semester and we knew that kids sometimes change their minds after they leave campus. It's a sort of buyer's remorse. So, we had Eric leave most of his belongings that he had brought on the visit. We thought if his stuff was here, he would be less likely to change his mind. Also, Coach Case went back to Macon with Eric. His instructions were to stay there until the week school started and to make sure Eric got on that plane to Oklahoma City. We had never done anything like this before. It was over the top, and it was expensive ... keeping Win on the road for three weeks. But we knew how valuable he would be for our team and for our university. We put all our eggs in the Eric Manuel basket, plus we truly believed this was Eric's best option moving forward. So, Win spent the last three weeks of the summer in Macon, Georgia hanging out with our new star player. Eric kept his word and got on the plane to Oklahoma City. He would become our best player but certainly not our only player. He couldn't do it by himself, but he gave our team a chance to be special. The other players embraced him. It was like having a celebrity around, but he didn't really want the limelight. He had all that at Kentucky and now he wanted to fit in, play ball, and just be one of the guys. School started and our players wanted to be in the gym. It was a time of pick-up games, and getting used to each other and the new teammates. It was clear in practices that Eric was a special player. But it was almost like he was holding back. He didn't want to be the center of attention anymore. What the NCAA did to Eric was not only unprecedented and unfair, but it was unconscionable. But Eric held no grudge, and he never talked about it. He was back playing basketball on his new team and was loving life again. It was a fresh start for the youngster from Georgia, and the air was filled with anticipation and excitement. We couldn't wait to start the season.

Everything wasn't exactly seashells and balloons with Eric's signing at OCU. As expected, there were media types all over the country who replayed the Kentucky scandal in its publications and broadcasts. Eric's story was big news in the sports world, and most of it was unfavorable. Some called him a cheater and a liar and even publicly questioned OCU's motive in granting him an athletic scholarship. Many other NAIA schools chose not to recruit Eric for this reason. They just did not need what they perceived as bad publicity. But OCU had a President who didn't back down from anyone. He was a fighter, and he vigorously defended the decision to allow Eric Manuel on our campus as a student-athlete. Dr. Walker did what he thought was in the best interest of the university. He was supportive of our intercollegiate sports programs and publicly took the offensive against those who painted a picture that OCU might have acted inappropriately or unethically in allowing Eric to continue his education and basketball eligibility at the school. He wasn't one to run and hide or succumb to public pressure. He did what he thought was right in the face of intense public scrutiny and criticism. Dr. Jerald Walker distinguished himself as a man of principle and integrity and I was proud to be on the same team.

    October rolled around and we were in the midst of practices in preparation for a November 4th start to the season. The team was working hard, the talent level was what we thought it would be, and there was an air of confidence that this team could be special. But a month before the season opener, we were blindsided by the NAIA national office in Kansas City. The chief administrator of the NAIA, Wally Schwartz, issued a press release to all NAIA member institutions in October 1990 saying that its eligibility committee had reviewed the Eric Manuel case and determined that Eric was INELIGIBLE for intercollegiate competition at any of its member schools. They had cited a rule that no student-athlete could be eligible for competition if their eligibility had been completed at another four-year school. The NAIA had determined that the NCAA lifetime ban for Eric was an emphatic example that Eric had completed his eligibility at Kentucky. Eric Manuel now seemed to be out of options to play college basketball. Even more importantly, Eric would not be able to complete his education, lacking the financial means to pay for college without an athletic scholarship. We were all caught by surprise with the NAIA ruling regarding Eric. It seemed that the NAIA had given in to pressure from other institutions, and also from the NCAA which appeared to want Eric Manuel punished for his alleged academic misdeeds. The ruling was unfair and had never been applied in this manner. But Eric's college career appeared to be over. Our team was devastated by the news. Not only had Eric established himself as our best player, but he had also endeared himself on campus by being a genuinely nice person, with no ego, just wanting to be treated like everyone else. I told Eric the news. It was beyond emotional and one of the hardest things I've ever had to do in my coaching career. We both cried. But it would get even tougher ... I had to call Mary and tell her the news that would absolutely break her spirit.

"I can do nothing on my own. As I hear, I judge, and my judgement is just, because I seek not my own will but the will of the one who sent me." John 5:30

CHAPTER 6 - SEEKING JUSTICE

Mary Manuel had entrusted her son with me and with Oklahoma City University. Now, I had to deliver the news that we were not able to follow through on our promises. Eric had been declared ineligible by the NAIA, and OCU would likely have to revoke his scholarship. Mary had a Godly faith that she relied on and that she preached to her boys. I shared her faith but neither of us understood why this was happening to Eric. I believe that my faith in 1990 was that of a child. I had made little effort to grow spiritually in my own life, much less be a Godly example for others. The truth that I now know, is that we are not made to understand God's ways and that God indeed has a plan for our life that supersedes our own plans. Through spiritual maturity, I have learned that His way is always better than mine. My wife Denna leaned on a much greater spiritual awareness than I did. When going through life's difficulties she would remind me that God always has a purpose. I thought maybe so, but he's not doing much for my coaching career. My reaction always seemed to revert back to my plans, my passion, my goals, and my purpose. It was an ideology of selfishness and part of the "me first" thought process. But at this very moment in time, my heart was breaking for Mary Manuel. Our team's championship potential was gone without Eric on the roster. I still had to coach the squad and give it my best effort, but we were beyond disappointed with the decision made by the NAIA about Eric's eligibility status. That evening, I made the phone call to Mary.

Mary cried when I gave her the news …out of sadness and worry for her son, but mostly because she just didn't understand. And I couldn't really explain it to her, because I didn't understand either. At the direction of President Walker, we had checked with NAIA headquarters before beginning our recruitment of Eric Manuel. Dr. Bud Sahmaunt, our athletic director, had spoken directly to the organization's head administrator, who gave him no reason to believe Eric would not be eligible as long as he met the requirements for transfer students. The NAIA's academic requirements were not as stringent as those of the NCAA. By its own bylaws, the NAIA required all student athletes to complete four years of eligibility in a total of ten semesters. For junior college transfers, they were not required to have obtained an associate's degree at the institution but rather needed only 48 transferable hours towards a degree, indicating satisfactory progress towards a four-year diploma. Eric had far surpassed all these requirements by receiving his associate's degree from Hiwassee. His hours and GPA were acceptable for all transfer students at OCU, so there was no special consideration given to Eric. He was accepted to the university based only on his merits and academic qualifications. However, the NAIA also had a clause stating that any student who had completed his or her eligibility at any four-year institution would be ineligible for further intercollegiate competition. The obvious intent of the rule was to prevent a player from playing four years at a school, then transferring and still having eligibility. But the NAIA was interpreting their own rule by saying Eric had completed his eligibility at Kentucky and therefore was ineligible. Eric's ACT test score had no bearing on his eligibility as a junior college transfer student according to both NAIA and NCAA regulations. They were trying to fit the square peg of the NCAA ban into the round hole of saying he had completed his eligibility at Kentucky, therefore making him ineligible. Their interpretation was a stretch at best because Eric had been in school for a total of six semesters and had played only two years of college basketball. The first year he played at Kentucky, then sat out a full season while the NCAA took its time investigating the matter for over a year, then played his second year of basketball at Hiwassee. This was affirmed by then-Kentucky Athletic Director C.M. Newton, who no longer had a dog in the fight. C.M. Newton was a highly respected former coach and current administrator at Kentucky when he wrote the following:

    In a letter dated Sept. 19, University of Kentucky athletic director C.M. Newton states, "*Eric did not complete his eligibility in varsity athletics at the University of Kentucky . . . It would appear to me that Eric should have two years of eligibility remaining.*" *An earlier letter written by Mr. Newton to the NAIA on Aug. 29 stated, "I urge you and the Eligibility Committee of the NAIA to immediately restore his eligibility to participate in varsity basketball. I am convinced Eric will be an excellent representative of the NAIA." (The Oklahoman News – Oct. 28, 1990).*

According to its own definition of "termination of eligibility" (article 4, section E, NAIA bylaws), it states, *"an athlete shall terminate his eligibility at the completion of either 10 semesters of attendance, four seasons of competition, or graduation."* None of these applied to Eric Manuel.

I asked Mary to give us a few days to try and sort through this. Again, she put her trust in me when I promised I would do everything I could to help Eric, having no idea what options he had left, if any. The next day I was summoned to a meeting with President Walker, Athletic Director Sahmaunt, and university counsel. Walker was visibly upset. Not at me, but at the NAIA for its treatment of Eric, and for the unfair and arbitrary nature of their decision. Walker would not take this lying down; he wanted to fight back. In the face of unfavorable national publicity shining on the face of our institution, OCU leadership took the side of a single student over the powerful NCAA and NAIA constituency. It was one of the most courageous things I'd ever seen from a college President, and more importantly ... it was the absolute right thing to do. Oklahoma City University has one of the best law schools in the country, and university-led attorneys got involved in Eric's case. However, the lead attorney was from outside the university. A bright, young rising star in the legal profession had read of Eric's plight and was sympathetic to his cause. Attorney Mark Hammons and his firm offered their services to Eric, pro bono.

The NCAA and the NAIA had long considered themselves as bulletproof from litigation under the self-applied umbrella that it was a "voluntary" organization, and its members could remove themselves from the organization at any time if they disagreed with policy or procedure. Their intention was to self-govern without any outside interference or oversight, and that included decisions and interpretations on eligibility. Hammons' strategy was to ask the court for injunctive relief, keeping the NAIA from interfering with Eric's scholarship agreement to play basketball at Oklahoma City University. Also named as a defendant in the case was the university itself, asking the court to validate and enforce OCU's scholarship agreement with Eric, in exchange for his participation in the university's intercollegiate athletic program. OCU was of course desirous of a decision favorable to Eric, which would allow him to remain on scholarship and retain his status as a student athlete. Hammons said in the pretrial conference,

"I feel excellent about the law. Our main contention is that you cannot unreasonably interfere with someone's right to contract and receive the benefits of his labor." (The Oklahoman, by Murray Evans – Oct. 11, 1990).

The Case was headed to trial and would be heard in Oklahoma County District Court, with Judge William Henderson presiding. The NAIA had its team of lawyers, and its prize witness, Wally Schwartz. Schwartz was the NAIA's vice president and was in charge of the organization's legislative services. He headed the eligibility committee which had voted to follow the NCAA's lead and ban Eric Manuel from playing at any of its member institutions. But Hammons had some heavyweight witnesses as well. He had sought to subpoena Sean Sutton as a witness since he had been present at the testing site when Eric took his second ACT test. Sean took the test for the second time as well on the same day. But Coach Eddie Sutton stepped in and asked Hammons for a favor. If he would leave Sean out of it, Eddie would himself testify on Eric's behalf. Eddie would be a compelling witness since he had been Eric's coach at Kentucky and was the one who had recruited him to play at UK. Eddie Sutton was a popular Oklahoma sports figure as well. Hammons agreed to exclude Sean from giving testimony. The elder Sutton testified that Eric Manuel was a "marvelous young man and an outstanding athlete." Regarding the ACT exam, Sutton said,

"To this day I still don't believe he did anything wrong. It's very likely something did happen on the test, but in my opinion, he knew nothing about it. I was shocked that the NAIA would not accept him. I feel there has to be compassion for him. It would be a great injustice if Eric Manuel was barred from playing college basketball." (Taken from court transcripts, Manuel vs NAIA).

Sutton further testified that Eric had the potential to be an NBA player, but that was unlikely to happen if he were not allowed to continue his college career. Hammons' next witness was Paul Hansen, my former boss and head coach at Oklahoma State University. He was now coaching at the University of Science and Arts of Oklahoma. He was also my mentor, one of my best friends, and the most honest man of integrity I had ever known. Coach

Hansen testified that based on his understanding of NAIA rules, Eric should have two years of eligibility remaining. He said that, in fact, recruiting services used by NAIA coaches highlight players who are ineligible for NCAA participation to focus on them for recruiting. He testified he was not aware of any NAIA by-law or rule that renders student-athletes, who are ineligible under NCAA rules, automatically ineligible under NAIA rules. What made this testimony so convincing was the fact that Paul's team at USAO was in our league and would have to play against Eric if he was eligible. A moment of levity in the courtroom occurred when Hammons asked Coach Hansen if he was reluctant to testify since his team might have to play against Eric. Hansen in his typical quick wit answered, "I've been beat by better." The courtroom erupted with laughter, including Judge Henderson. Paul Hansen stood up for me, and for Eric Manuel, and told the truth perhaps to his own detriment. By doing so, he was displaying the highest level of character and integrity imaginable. This was Paul Hansen. Paul passed away a few years later, and my son Derek Paul, is named after him. He represented everything that was good about college athletics. Win and I both testified, as did other OCU staffers and administrators. But it was the testimony of Paul Hansen and Eddie Sutton that was the most compelling for Eric's case.

Lawyers for the NAIA put on their witnesses, most notably Mr. Wallace Schwartz. The primary point from Schwartz on the stand was that Eric had completed his eligibility at Kentucky when he was given the lifetime ban by the NCAA. But he admitted that he did not want the NAIA to be seen as a dumping ground for players who had issues at an NCAA school. A moment of serious drama encapsulated the courtroom when my assistant, Win Case, stood to his feet during NAIA witness testimony, pointing his finger at the witness and yelling out, "liar." Win, of course, was admonished by the judge, but this was an indication of his passion for Eric and for the stress and pressure of the situation. It was hard for all of us to sit quietly and listen when the other side would spin the facts of the case to coincide with their agenda, or just blatantly fabricate their testimony. The NAIA was pulling out all the stops in its quest to keep Manuel from ever playing again. Through the years Wally Schwartz has won numerous awards for exemplary service to college athletics and to the NAIA. He may have done a lot of good in the area of college sports, but this was certainly not his finest moment. For whatever reason, it seemed like this was personal for Schwartz.

"Schwartz concedes that the NAIA weighed another factor—Manuel's status as a pariah. "Some of our concern is image," he says. "We don't want to be seen as an organization of last resort. You can imagine that headlines like MANUEL BANNED, CAN ONLY PLAY NAIA don't make us look very good. We don't have a vendetta against Eric Manuel. We just don't think as an organization that the young man fits our definition of a student-athlete." (Sports Illustrated, 2-11-91)

But there were many examples of players transferring from NCAA schools to NAIA institutions that had experienced academic problems, issues with law enforcement, or other violations of school and/or community standards. Eric testified at trial that his grades at UK had been acceptable, he had never been in any trouble, had not been suspended by the university, and he did not cheat on his ACT test. The truth is, that regardless of Schwartz's testimony and his wholesome desire for the NAIA, many NAIA schools have been a haven for kids needing a second chance due to academic issues or some type of misconduct.

The trial lasted 4 days when both sides rested, and Judge Henderson recessed to take the case under advisement. He would study the facts of the case, which included a quick education on the NAIA and NCAA rule books. Judge William Henderson would alone decide Eric's fate. It was on Friday, October 26th, 1990, we received word that Judge Henderson had made his decision. All the parties quickly reassembled back in the courtroom. The room was jam-packed with attorneys for all sides, OCU personnel, supporters and other interested parties. This case had brought national attention to OCU, whether it was wanted or not. Outside the courtroom, there was a throng of reporters and TV cameras waiting for the court's decision. Judge Henderson entered the courtroom and asked everyone to be seated.

"I have read the rules they (the NAIA) were using and they simply did not apply to Eric Manuel. I have required them to do certain things, mainly not to interfere with Mr. Manuel's present scholarship contract." (Court transcripts, Manuel vs NAIA).

The Court had issued a permanent injunction that allowed Eric Manuel to continue his basketball career at Oklahoma City University without interference from the NAIA. Henderson went on to say that Manuel would potentially suffer irreparable harm if he were barred from playing basketball by the NAIA. There was both elation and relief by most of those inside the courtroom. Eric had won. OCU had also won. NAIA lead attorney Dell Gordon said afterward that the NAIA would most certainly appeal the decision to the Oklahoma Supreme Court. But for now, Eric Manuel could play. He never asked for special consideration or privileges. He never sought money or damages. All he wanted was to have the opportunity to play this game that he loved. Eric's only comment after the trial was, "It'll be good to get back on the court and do something you love to do." This was Eric Manuel, avoiding the limelight and media attention. He just wanted to play.

We met with the media briefly and then all left the courthouse and headed back to campus. The team had started practice with Coach Case and hadn't heard the news yet. Someone had given me a "re-elect Judge Henderson" campaign sign and I held it up as Eric and I walked back into the gym shoulder to shoulder. What resulted was the biggest mob scene and celebratory dog pile I had ever witnessed. There was jubilant yelling and screaming, hugging and chanting from Eric's teammates. They knew this decision could vault us to a championship-caliber team, but the celebration was mostly because they loved Eric as a friend and as a valued teammate. And all had compassion for what he had been through. We canceled the rest of the practice that day. This was Eric's time. This was Eric's day, and he just wanted to share it with his team. I let them all have this time together and quietly retired in solitude to my office. I had a phone call to make. It was one that I relished on this most joyous occasion. My heart was pounding with excitement as I made the call to Mary Manuel.

"And with joy before him, let's run the race marked out for us."
Hebrews 12:1

CHAPTER 7 - DOWN TO BUSINESS

When I called Mary to give her the news that the NAIA had declared her son ineligible to play basketball, she openly wept. On this day Mary cried again, but this time it was tears of joy followed by a chorus of "Praise the Lord and Thank you, Jesus." Mary had entrusted me with the welfare of her son. I had made promises ... and now was able to make good on them. The start of our season was little more than a week away, and Eric Manuel would be in the starting lineup. It was a fresh start for Eric and the beginning of a new chapter in my coaching career at OCU.

Amazingly, Eric and Mary held no bitterness towards those who tried to derail him from ever playing college basketball again. Instead, there was nothing but joyous anticipation with a new season, at a new school, and a promising future. There was a positive buzz on campus and in the community that was tempered by more negative publicity surrounding the court's decision. The NAIA did in fact eventually file an appeal with the Oklahoma Supreme Court. The organization's chief administrator Wally Schwartz issued a release that said in part, "the crux of the matter is whether or not the association will be allowed to administer and enforce its own rules, or whether the courts are going to do it for us." This was a bit of a departure from their primary points made during trial testimony. They had tried to apply the rule for "completion of eligibility" to Eric's situation which was a bad strategy and ultimately failed them at trial. Now in their appeal, it appeared they were trying to drive home the point that the NAIA was a voluntary organization, and they were not required to follow any kind of due process towards its members or their student-athletes. But regardless of their strategy, it was likely that Eric would graduate from OCU before ever getting a ruling from the court. So, Eric was safe to compete for the next two years. But if they won their appeal, OCU could face sanctions down the road for playing an ineligible player. Ultimately the NAIA saw the futility of their case against Eric and dropped the appeal. I'll likely never understand the motivation behind the NCAA and NAIA attempts to ban Eric Manuel from ever playing again, or for making him the scapegoat of the scandal at Kentucky. But I am proud of the manner in which OCU went to bat for this kid. President Walker was an absolute all-star and OCU's legal defense team had been stellar. Outside counsel for Eric led by Mark Hammons was top-notch and covered all the bases while presenting a most convincing and compelling case. Eric, and the rest of the OCU community, will forever be in his debt. So many people came to Eric's defense because they saw what Dr. Walker saw, "a decent human being that studies hard." But some of our competitors and rivals didn't like the fact that we fought, and won, against the NAIA. When the President of one of our district foes wrote a letter to the editor of the state's largest newspaper, critical of OCU's support of Eric, Dr. Walker responded with his own letter.

To the Sports Editor: This open letter is in response to letters printed under the headline "OCU Incident Not Indicative of NAIA" in the Oct. 21 edition of The Oklahoman. Within the text of the two letters were several errors and misstatements of facts that need to be cleared up.

I believe it is important to understand that while Oklahoma City University supports the contention of Eric Manuel that he is eligible to participate in intercollegiate athletics organized and supervised by the NAIA, the university is not the plaintiff in the suit under consideration in Oklahoma District Court. The university is, in fact, listed as a defendant in the lawsuit, which was filed by Mr. Manuel against both OCU and the NAIA in an effort to establish his eligibility. In addition, the university in no way wishes to be placed in the position of defending the article written by John Rohde and published by The Oklahoman on Oct. 4. To begin with, the letter written by the president of Northwestern refers to OCU as a "short-term and non-representative member" of the NAIA. Yes, OCU may be non-representative, particularly because of the small amount it spends on its athletic programs when compared to many colleges and universities holding membership in the NAIA or the NCAA. We may be non-representative of a number of NAIA and NCAA schools in that our freshmen's test scores consistently rank high among schools in the southwest region. We may be non-representative because our academic standards are more competitive than many NAIA and NCAA member institutions.

The president of Northwestern makes several statements concerning the actual case currently before the courts. Unfortunately, his statements do not accurately reflect court testimony or the NAIA rulebook.

According to the letter, "That (NAIA) rule clearly states that any student who is not eligible at a four-year school from which he transfers cannot be eligible in the NAIA." In truth, the rule (Article 5, Section E.4 of the NAIA Official Handbook) actually states, "A student who has completed eligibility at a four-year institution is ineligible for further intercollegiate participation." According to the NAIA's own definition of termination of eligibility (also found in Article 4, Section E), an athlete shall terminate his eligibility at the completion of either 10 semesters of attendance, four seasons of competition or graduation, none of which apply to Mr. Manuel.

Furthermore, in a letter dated Sept. 19, University of Kentucky athletic director C.M. Newton states, "Eric did not complete his eligibility in varsity athletics at the University of Kentucky . . . It would appear to me that Eric should have two years of eligibility remaining." I believe his statement of Eric's eligibility satisfies the requirements of Article 5, Section E, in regard to eligibility. An earlier letter written by Mr. Newton to the NAIA on Aug. 29 stated, "I urge you and the Eligibility Committee of the NAIA to immediately restore his eligibility to participate in varsity basketball. I am convinced Eric will be an excellent representative of the NAIA."

According to court testimony, several athletes currently compete for or have competed at NAIA institutions despite their lack of eligibility at NCAA institutions with which they have been previously identified. If the intent of this rule is to prevent such athletes from competing, then the NAIA may be forced to declare several athletes ineligible for future competition. Because the rule has not been applied in such a manner, athletes have been able to compete for NAIA schools, many with great success.

The letter from the president of Northwestern states that "When OCU coaches were recruiting Mr. Manuel, they asked the national office for a ruling and were told he would not be eligible." To begin with, if the coaches at OCU had asked the national office for a clarification of Mr. Manuel's status, they would have been in clear violation of the stated national office policy that requires the athletic director or faculty athletic representative of the institution to make the inquiry. Before the recruiting process involving Mr. Manuel began, the athletic director of OCU called the national office to inquire about Mr. Manuel's status. The athletic director was told only to be cautious of the suspension rule, suspension from a previous school. After establishing Mr. Manuel's eligibility under this rule, the university gave permission to its basketball coaches to begin the recruitment of the prospective student athlete. The letter states, "OCU may not like the rule, but the fact is OCU agreed to abide by this and other NAIA rules when it sought the benefits of membership." OCU abides by the rules of the association and will continue to do so. However, every NAIA institution is able to appeal a rule on the basis of an exceptional ruling, and many institutions find it necessary to do this during each academic year. It was stated that the salient rule in this case has been on the books since before 1968, without challenge. It has also never been interpreted or applied as it has been in the Manuel case. This constitutes, from my perspective, arbitrary and capricious action.

The letter closes with the statement that the president of Northwestern hopes John Rohde will be fair and accurate when he chooses to write about the NAIA in the future. Our profound hope is that the president will be as fair and accurate the next time he chooses to write a letter to the editor or author other public documents.

The second letter under the same heading came from the executive director of the NAIA, and again I find myself baffled by the misstatements found within its text. The most glaring is that he says, "According to officials from the University of Kentucky, Mr. Manuel does not have the eligibility remaining at the institution." As I have already pointed out, the University of Kentucky athletic director has a written letter stating that Mr. Manuel did not complete his athletic eligibility at that school. The executive director also points out the NAIA's attention to academic standards is exemplified by association rules that are more stringent than NCAA rules. OCU believes in high academic standards for all its students, and the university has refused admission to more than one athlete who subsequently enrolled in another NAIA institution and competed against the Chiefs and the Lady Chiefs. Eric Manuel meets the academic standards set forth by the university's Student Handbook, and, in fact, has a solid academic record at both previous institutions of attendance.

Taken together, the two letters represent a haphazard attempt *to report the facts of the Eric Manuel case. Equally awkward was the handling of Eric's eligibility case, particularly as it relates to the National Eligibility Committee's review process. During the recent court hearing, the chairman of the NAIA National Eligibility Committee, Arleigh Dodson of Lewis and Clark College in Oregon, admitted in testimony that the NAIA based its determination of Mr. Manuel's lack of eligibility on a press release only and did not ask the University of Kentucky about his status for future eligibility. Two decisions regarding Mr. Manuel's eligibility were made by the NAIA before officials of that association contacted the University of Kentucky. OCU is not the only source of support for Mr. Manuel in his court action. Among those testifying on his behalf during the court hearing were Eddie Sutton, his former coach at the University of Kentucky who is now head coach at Oklahoma State, and Paul Hansen, head coach at USAO. I find it impressive that coach Hansen, whom I consider an individual of impeccable integrity, spoke on Eric's behalf, particularly when you consider that his school is a member of the same conference as OCU and will have to face the Chiefs at least twice during the upcoming season.*

My purpose in writing this letter has been to set the record straight about the facts surrounding the eligibility case of Eric Manuel. It is imperative that education leaders provide examples of clarity and accuracy in their public statements.

Jerald C. Walker
President of Oklahoma City University
(The Oklahoman, 10-28-90)

Walker was a true leader and never backed away from a fight. Especially when the other side did not do their homework or have their facts straight. But few would take such an open and public adversarial position against a fellow contemporary. Regardless of what happened with our season, I was proud of our campus leadership and to work for the best college administrator I had ever known. He was a man of courage and integrity and an absolute champion. But now we needed to shift our focus to the season, which was just days away.

We knew we were good, but the team had some flaws. Eric was our biggest starter at 6'6 and was mostly a perimeter player. Our center, Mark Chambers, had played for Abe Lemons during Abe's last season and was effective but way undersized for his position at only 6'4. Junior college transfer Tony Terrell from San Jacinto was our point guard but was also undersized at 5'10. But "San Jac" as it was commonly referred to, was a powerhouse junior college program and Tony had played against some of the best players in the country. Sharpshooter Mike McCoy had played for Win at Eastern Oklahoma Junior College, and our starting five was rounded out by surprise starter Michael Berry, who had started his college career as a walk-on. Both McCoy and Berry stood around 6'3, so we were definitely a small team. But Eric made everyone better and would be the focus of most opposing defenses. He would see his share of double teams, so we needed everyone else to step up. Our bench was strong, with mostly starters from the previous year. We played in the Sooner Athletic Conference, and our District was comprised of 16 teams, all from Oklahoma, and was regarded as perhaps the strongest NAIA district in the country. What made our district even tougher this year was that Oral Roberts University had dropped down to the NAIA level from NCAA division one and competed in our district, while retaining all of their players who had been recruited as D-1 players. In order to get a berth in the National tournament in Kansas City, teams had to win their district championship outright. There were no at-large teams that made the tournament. Every team in the national tournament will have won their respective district championship in order to qualify for nationals. And with ORU now in the mix for District 9 honors, it would be a challenging road to Kansas City. With a sixteen-team district, only one could make the national tournament.

  We started the season 6-0 in dominant fashion with an average win margin of 31 points per game. But our early schedule had obviously not been particularly strong, and things would definitely get tougher. Our next game would be on the road with NCAA member, Cameron University. They matched us athletically and were much bigger along their front line. We lost the game 95-90, which was our first of the season and my first loss as OCU's head coach. Our players were embarrassed by the loss and came back the next game with a vengeance winning by 60 over LeTourneau University. Our next game would be at home facing Oral Roberts University. ORU featured one of the top scorers in the nation at any level of college basketball. Greg Sutton hailed from Oklahoma City Douglass High School, so this game was more than just another game for him and provided a little extra personal motivation. The game was being touted with each team having a potential first-round NBA draft pick. Sutton and Manuel would go head-to-head, and the match-up was highly anticipated with a sold-out, standing-room-only crowd in Frederickson Field house. The game did not disappoint, and the two stars were beyond magnificent. Sutton was unstoppable setting a school single-game scoring record, as well as a District 9 record with 68 points. We double-teamed him, face-guarded him and tried a box and one defense but nothing phased him. It was the single best performance by an opponent in my entire coaching career. Eric was great as well, scoring 40 points and grabbing 14 rebounds. The 40 points was a single point shy of an all-time OCU record. But the most important stat was the final score, with the Chiefs hanging on for a 116-114 overtime victory. The packed crowd had been treated to one of the greatest games in OCU history, an absolute classic, as well as individual performances by two of the best ever to play in the NAIA. And with the win over ORU, we had pretty much solidified our status as the team to beat and the District Nine favorite.

The team reeled off another six straight wins after the ORU game before the rematch with the Titans up the Turner Turnpike in Tulsa. I'm sure ORU relished the opportunity to get their revenge, especially on their home floor. Sutton had continued his scoring dominance, but ORU now had a new player who became eligible at the end of the first semester. Sebastian Neal was a 6'6 forward who had transferred to ORU from the University of Georgia and was considered another potential NBA talent. We were still finding our way as a team, but we were pleasantly surprised as a coaching staff. We knew Eric was good, but we didn't know how unselfish he was. He was the ultimate team player, which of course further endeared him to his teammates. Eric was obviously our best player, but we had five players averaging in double figures. It just made us harder to beat, and when Eric drew double teams, other guys were stepping up and could pick up the slack. ORU would be hard to beat a second time, especially on their home floor.

Another packed crowd showed up for the game, this time at the Mabee Center on ORU's campus which seated crowds of over 11,000. Every seat was filled for the rematch between District 9's two best teams. The first game between the two teams and been one for the ages. Rarely does the sequel live up to the hype of the first game. And true to form, with less than 10 minutes left in the game, we held a 15-point lead against the home team. It looked like it might be a runaway but ORU's Sutton caught fire, and he and Neal showed why there were several NBA scouts in attendance. But we held off the rally and won the game by a bucket, 104-102. Eric had a stellar 29 points and 16 rebounds, while Sutton scored 46. It was a game that equaled the drama and tension of the first game, but we had just enough to head back down the turnpike with our eighth straight win.

Our next game was another rematch ... this time with Cameron, an NCAA team. We had lost the earlier meeting, but I thought we had a better team. But it was scheduled for only two days after the ORU game, and our guys were physically drained. We dropped the Cameron game by 2 points in a lackluster effort. This was obviously a non-district game and wouldn't affect the season much, but still disappointing. We came back and won four straight before losing to NCAA Division One member Colorado State on the road. This was a guarantee game which meant they paid us a handsome stipend to come play a game on their home court without a return game. We played poorly and lost badly to Colorado State, but the remainder of the season was what was really important. We were coming down the home stretch with eight district games remaining before the playoffs. We seemed to be hitting our stride at just the right time and won our final eight games. We had finished the regular season with a record of 27-3 and were playing at a high level entering the postseason. Eric had easily been our best player, but our scoring attack was balanced, with any one of our top six or seven players capable of leading us in scoring on any given night. But in our last eight contests, Eric had led us in scoring in only half the games. The other guys were improving and showing that this was certainly not a one-man show.

We entered the postseason as the #1 seed in District 9, and it looked like we might be headed for a game three with #2 seed Oral Roberts in the finals. It didn't much matter what we had done in our season up to this point, we needed to win three straight games to punch our ticket to Kansas City for the national tournament. There were no losers bracket or consolation winners, and there were no at-large bids for nationals. One loss now and your season was over. We won our first two district tournament games pretty easily, and as predicted, would face ORU for the district championship on March 6th. We had defeated ORU twice during the regular season, but both times by only a two-point margin. It would be tough to win a third time, especially with our whole season at stake and against the most talented team we would play all year. Greg Sutton was averaging 35 points per game and led the nation in scoring, while Sebastian Neal led the nation in rebounding with over 18 per game. Our records going into the finals were almost identical. We were 29-3 and ORU was 29-5, with both teams ranked in the top 5 nationally.

"Shootout III" it was called, and the game was close as we thought it would be. Sutton was his usual spectacular self, but Neal was just as good. We led by 4 at halftime but the game was tied 85-85 midway through the second half, when our guys put the hammer down and went on a 9-0 scoring run. Sutton scored 41 points before fouling out late in the game and we went on to a 117-104 championship win. Eric scored 26 but Mark Chambers took over in the second half finishing with 19 points and 10 rebounds. Our guards, Tony Terrell and Mike McCoy were spectacular as well. Sebastian Neal scored 25 points with 12 boards for ORU. Having beaten ORU three times, we were District 9 champions and on our way to Kansas City for the national tournament. And we were playing our best basketball of the season having won eleven straight games.

Unlike the NCAA tournament, the NAIA plays its tournament at one location (Kemper Arena in Kansas City) in a total of six days. We entered the tournament as the #2 overall national seed and would have to win five games in less than a week to bring home a National Championship. It was an endurance contest to say the least. OCU had never won a national championship in men's basketball at any level. But here we were at nationals, with 31 other district champions, and had as good a chance as anyone of bringing home the trophy.

As the #2 seed it meant that we played seed #31. One would think this should be the easiest game we would likely play, but it was anything but. In what Eric Manuel described after the game as "the worst we've played all year," we came out with a narrow 3-point win against Concordia (Nebraska). They had two chances to tie at the buzzer but missed both attempts. We were incredibly close to being one and done in the national tournament, but we couldn't dwell on it. We had less than 24 hours to prepare for our next game, against Concord (West Virginia), which should be an even tougher opponent.

As most agree, District Nine was perhaps the strongest NAIA competition in the country. The next couple of games proved that to be true, as we defeated Concord and St. Mary's (Michigan) by 22 and 18 points respectively, which vaulted us into the semifinals. Mark Chambers continued his dominance as an undersized center, scoring 28 points in each of the two games. We were one game away from the title game, with only Pfeiffer College (North Carolina) standing in our way. Pfeiffer was coached by Bobby Lutz who later capped a great career with head coaching stints at a couple of Division One schools, North Carolina State and Charlotte. Pfeiffer looked like a high major type of team and was much bigger than we were, played super physical, and matched us athletically. For the first time in the national tournament, we were behind at halftime … Pfeiffer led 47-44. The second half was a back-and-forth game with 11 lead changes. But at around the nine-minute mark of the second half our defense took over, keeping Pfeiffer scoreless for more than five minutes. We shot the lights out from that point and finished on top 100-85. But the physicality of Pfeiffer had taken its toll. Center Mark Chambers caught an elbow and needed five stitches after the game and point guard Tony Terrell had a laceration over his eye that took seven stitches. Tony had left the game to get sutured up but came back to lead us in scoring with 21 points. This was so indicative of the toughness and competitiveness of this team. We were banged up but headed to play for the NAIA national championship, after finally getting a very needed day off. Even with the injuries, our players had an unbelievable resolve about them, and everyone would be available for the title game. They weren't about to miss this opportunity, which was a dream come true for the players. This team had developed a chemistry that was unmatched. They were unselfish to a man, didn't much care who got the credit, and loved the game and loved each other. If there was ever a team that deserved to win a championship it was these guys. I was just proud to be along for the ride. But we had one more game, this time against Central Arkansas which has a history as an NCAA division one school and where Scottie Pippen of Chicago Bulls fame had played his college ball. They had a Hall of Fame coach in Don Dyer and had breezed through their side of the bracket. We spent the day off watching game films, and we couldn't find any weaknesses to try and exploit. They were big, athletic, and had shooters at pretty much every position. We were smaller, but I believed in my team, and they had proven themselves over and over.

The championship game was televised nationally on ESPN, which in 1991, was a much bigger deal than it is today, with almost every major sporting event being televised. Our players were exhausted and beat up, but excited and running on high adrenaline. It came down to one game for all the marbles, and with a victory, would be OCU's first-ever national championship in men's basketball. Central Arkansas would be formidable, but I had never seen our guys so hyped up for a game. My concern would be if we got too emotional at the beginning and then ran out of gas as the game wore on … which is exactly what happened. We sprinted out of the gate to a big lead and settled into a comfortable eight-point lead at halftime. We built our biggest lead of the game early in the second half, 44-33, but fatigue and the overall health of our team was concerning. Central Arkansas battled back and with eight minutes remaining, we held a one-point lead, 62-61. Our guys were giving everything they had but there wasn't much left in the tank. We then scored six straight points to give ourselves some breathing room, but there was no quit in UCA. The rest of the game was tight, and we led by three, 77-74, in the waning moments of regulation. We threw an interception from out of bounds with three seconds left and they had one final chance to tie the game. But the desperation three-point attempt was off target and the celebration began. The Oklahoma City University Chiefs had won its first-ever NATIONAL CHAMPIONSHIP!

"Do not lay up for yourselves treasures on earth, for lay up for yourselves treasures in heaven." Matthew 6:19

CHAPTER 8 - HAIL TO THE CHIEFS

The best part of winning a national championship was the fact that I was just so incredibly happy for Eric Manuel. He had been named the MVP of the tournament and had to be feeling a small amount of redemption. Every road game of the season there would be chants of A-C-T coming from the student section at periodic times in the game. Eric never responded or showed emotion. It had to bother him, but he said it actually motivated him. He had been through so much, just to have the privilege to play this game that he loved so much. OCU was a far cry from the likes of Kentucky and the other schools that were recruiting him out of high school. But he truly didn't care ... he knew he was a part of something special. The people at OCU embraced and loved him because Eric was just one of them. There was no pretend about this kid, he was deliriously happy and fulfilled with where he was, with the closeness he felt towards his teammates, and the school that had fought so hard for him. He was finally at peace.

Fans, students, and supporters who had not gone to Kansas City met us at the field house when we arrived on campus for an impromptu pep rally the day after the championship game. But the players were exhausted and just wanted to crash. After a few minutes of celebrating and raising the trophy, we all dispersed and went our separate ways. These guys had in fact made history. They were beaming with pride, having accomplished what they set out to do. We all needed to rest for a few days, and then it was back to work. Win and I were already thinking about next year, and the holes in the roster we needed to fill after losing a couple of key players to graduation.

Denna had been our biggest fan and my greatest supporter throughout my career. With our son Derek just a toddler, her top priority changed to being a mom. She was still involved, rarely missed a game, and was still working full-time. Her plate was full, and I was not much help. We were growing apart and I did nothing to stop it. I was too involved in my work to have much time for family and was always focused on the next game, the next season, and recruiting. Success oftentimes breeds opportunity. With the championship behind us, an eye-popping record of 35-3, and prospects looking bright for next year, I had never been more excited about my career. And others noticed. The University of Tulsa was looking for a new basketball coach, and I got the call from athletic director, Rick Dixon. I had played college ball at Tulsa and Rick was playing football at the same time. We had been friends for quite some time, and now I was on their short list of coaching candidates to replace outgoing coach J.D. Barnett. The idea of coaching at Tulsa was exhilarating, especially since I had played there, and it would be a huge career jump from OCU. I interviewed with Dixon, and it went great. In the end, he told me I had the job, but he needed to interview a minority candidate. I was making plans for the move to Tulsa. Denna's parents lived there, and I'd be working for a friend in Dixon. I already had put a staff together as well. Tulsa was the hometown of Win Case, and he would leave OCU to come with me. My brother Phil had been an assistant for J.D. and agreed to stay. And my third assistant would be my mentor and closest friend, Paul Hansen. Paul was in his 60s now and was having some health issues. But he wanted to come, and we were all super excited about the idea of coaching together at Tulsa. A few days later I got the call from Dixon and could tell something was wrong. They were going in a different direction and had offered the job to the assistant coach at Kentucky, Tubby Smith. Smith had accepted. We were all disappointed but had to get over it quickly. Another opportunity arose when I got a call from Southwest Texas State, which is now just called Texas State. They were looking for a new coach and I was on their list. In a twist of fate, the two finalists for the job ended up being myself, and my lifelong friend Jim Wooldridge, who was coaching at Central Missouri. Wooldridge and I had played with Alvan Adams on the best high school team Oklahoma has ever produced. Putnam City High School had won the state championship in 1972 with a perfect 26-0 record. Jim and I were juniors on that team, and Alvan was a senior. Adams went on to play at the University of Oklahoma, was drafted by the Phoenix Suns, and became the NBA's rookie of the year after leaving OU. Alvan is still the second-leading scorer in Suns history behind Walter Davis. But Wooldridge and I had been best friends throughout high school and played in a couple of all-star games together. He went on to play at

Louisiana Tech before starting his coaching career. He had great success at Central Missouri, and now we were interviewing for the same job at Southwest Texas and on campus at the same time. The administration and selection committee had no idea we even knew each other, but we were comparing notes the entire time in the hiring process. After the interview, the school offered me the job and I accepted. It was an NCAA Division One school and a step up from OCU, and another rung on the ladder of the upward career climb. I got back to campus at OCU and scheduled a meeting with Dr. Walker. He knew I would have opportunities after the season we just had, and he was prepared. Walker offered me a hefty raise in salary to stay at OCU, with some other benefits including a new car. And the truth was, I was really happy there. Not to mention that we were on a 16-game winning streak with a good team coming back that included the tournament MVP and the best NAIA player in the country. A major factor was also that I just didn't feel right leaving these kids, especially Eric with everything he had gone through. After talking with Denna, I had a change of heart and decided to stay with the Chiefs. I called the athletic director in Texas and told him I had changed my mind and then called Walker and told him we were staying. We were still fresh off our championship, but the extended season had put us behind in recruiting. We had to get busy.

We were losing our second-best player and center, Mark Chambers, as well as another starter in Michael Berry. But we had a couple of major college transfers on the squad who were redshirting because of the transfer rules. They could practice with the team but weren't eligible for competition until the fall semester. The best player we had sitting out was Darrin Terry, who had transferred from Texas A&M. Terry was a 6'6 phenom athlete who would likely take Chambers' spot at center. But we still needed size, and another point guard. We signed Keith Stewart, a 6'9 D-1 transfer from the University of Idaho. He was the legit big guy we needed inside. We had targeted the point guard we wanted ... another D-1 transfer, this time from the University of Oklahoma, Smokey McCovery. Smokey was a starter at OU, but I think had gotten sideways with someone on the coaching staff. He had averaged 11 points per game for the Sooners, which ended up ranked as the #1 team in the nation at the end of the regular season. He was looking to leave, and we were the perfect fit. He was a senior with just one year of eligibility remaining but should fit in nicely with the team we had coming back. Smokey signed with us in early summer, and we were set. In fact, we were loaded with talent ... maybe even more than the team that had just won the national championship. With the roster we had assembled, we would become the prohibitive preseason favorites to repeat as national champions.

Most coaches do their best to lower team expectations in public settings. I've done it all of my career. If fans and supporters are expecting championships, there is obviously a higher chance of disappointment. And I was cautionary at our preseason press conference but admitted the talent level of our team was special. My only cause for concern was our team chemistry, which had carried us to the national championship. We had some glue guys that held us together that were lost to graduation. This season we were loaded with seniors, and I was concerned not only about chemistry but also about our team concept. Last year, our players accepted roles and played with amazing selflessness. Would a senior-laden team play with the same "team first" attitude that propelled us to a championship last year? It was really the only thing that could stop us. If we had that intangible and stayed healthy, there's no reason we couldn't do it again. And that was my message at the preseason presser. I didn't downplay our potential or abilities, because almost everyone knew we were loaded.

We had an all-division one transfer starting five. Eric was still our best overall player, but McCovery, McCoy, Terrell, Terry, and Stewart were all capable of carrying us on a given night. We tried hard to get Division One teams on our schedule, but no one would bite. We were an NAIA school but likely good enough to make the NCAA Division 1 tournament. There wasn't much to gain by playing us and a whole lot to lose. Oral Roberts University had made our schedule a bit easier, as they moved back to NCAA Division 1 for the 1991-92 season. They had no desire to continue the series with OCU after losing three straight to us the previous season. We had finished last season on a 16-game winning streak en route to the national title, so the streak would continue until our first loss.

We breezed through the early part of our schedule and weren't really tested. Heading into the Christmas break we had won our first 12 games, and 28 in a row dating back to last season. The first real test came on January 4th, in a rematch with NCAA member Cameron University, who had swept us in two games the previous year. We trailed by a point, 39-38 at halftime, before blowing it open in the second half winning 91-75. The next game was a rematch of the championship game with Central Arkansas from 1991. UCA had scheduled us thinking the title game had been a fluke and wanted revenge. We won this one too, 80-70, in a close contest before starting conference games in mid-January. We were undefeated, ranked #1 in the nation in the NAIA, and on a serious roll. Manuel had been dominant, and Smokey McCovery was a big, strong guard who was an absolute defensive stopper. Mike McCoy was draining three-pointers as our best perimeter shooter and Darrin Terry had made up for the graduation of Mark Chambers. But this team had become dominant on the defensive end. Smokey would defend the opposition's best perimeter player, and this year we had some rim protection with a legit big man in the middle, 6'9 Keith Stewart who had transferred from the University of Idaho. Eric could guard any position, so we were strong on both ends of the floor. We were balanced and my preseason concerns about chemistry and team concept were alleviated. These kids loved to play and just wanted to win. We had no real weaknesses, and they played hard and played together. We pretty much waltzed through the conference part of the schedule and remained undefeated going into the District 9 playoffs with a record of 30-0, and on a winning streak of 46 straight.

As the top seed in the playoffs, we would play #8 Phillips University in the first round. We beat Phillips by 40 and would play Northeastern Oklahoma in the district semifinals. NSU was coached by Ken Hayes who had been my college coach at Tulsa. We were great friends, and he was a top-notch coach, having been the head coach at Tulsa, Oral Roberts and New Mexico State before finishing his career at Northeastern. But coaching wouldn't matter in this game as NSU was totally outmanned. We won easily 101-72. This set up the District Finals against the #2 seed, Northwestern Oklahoma. We had beaten them decisively earlier in the season, but now the winner of this game would get the automatic bid to the national tournament in Kansas City. Coach Bob Battisti was a defensive-minded coach at Northwestern, and he engineered a game plan against us that had me scared. This was a time before the shot clock was introduced into college basketball and Battisti had his team hold the ball, using delay tactics. I hated the fact he did this to us because, in the back of my mind, I thought this might be the way to beat us. But we turned up the pressure on the defensive end and forced some turnovers. In the end, our team was just better than they were, and in the lowest-scoring game of the season, we came out on top 53-43 and were on our way back to Kansas City. The game plan for Battisti was genius, considering the disparity in raw talent, and I was afraid other teams might be watching and would try to use the same concept to take us down. It was now back to a single elimination tournament at nationals. One bad night, one loss, and the season was over. But we entered the national tournament as the #1 overall seed, the top-ranked team in the country, and on a 49-game winning streak. Expectations were such that anything short of another championship would be a failure. All the pressure was squarely on our team, and we would get every opponent's best shot and best effort in Kansas City.

First up was Columbia Union University out of Maryland. They were the lowest seed in the tournament, but I reminded our team of the close call we had last year in the first round against a lower-seeded squad. They apparently paid attention because we won the opener in a blowout, 107-73. The guys seemed to relish being the hunted and took pride in being the undefeated defending national champions. Our second-round opponent was Urbana University from Ohio and the game was a close one. We didn't play our best but were still good enough to win, 96-89. We had always bounced back pretty strong after a close call and the next game against Cumberland (Kentucky) was no exception, winning 97-63. This set up a rematch of last year's semifinal matchup with Pfeiffer University from North Carolina. Pfeiffer was still coached by Bobby Lutz and he had a team that was a close match with our talent level. They were bigger than we were across the front line and equaled our athleticism and depth. Tony Smith was the leading three-point shooter in the country, and Antonio Harvey, a seven-foot transfer from the University of Georgia was formidable inside. I thought this would be a tough matchup for us and it was. We were up by only five at halftime, 51-46. In a back-and-forth affair, we pulled away late in the game winning 102-92, putting us back into the national championship game. Mike McCoy and Smokey McCovery had scored 25 points each, proving once again that we were anything but a one-man team. The defense was a big factor as we had 11 steals in the game. Our opponent for the national championship game would be a familiar foe … the University of Central Arkansas who we had beaten in the previous title game a year ago.

We had played 4 games in 4 days and needed the day off prior to the national finals. We were tired but healthy and UCA's side of the bracket had been grueling as well. They had won only a single game by double digits in the tournament ... every game had been a dogfight. But they had survived each, and having lost to us in last year's final, and also in a regular season game this season, they were hungry and motivated. The incentive was there for UCA, and many thought they were a team of destiny, having won so many tight games during the tournament. I thought it was vitally important for us to establish a lead early, not letting them hang around in striking distance to have an opportunity for late-game heroics. But when you've won 53 games in a row your confidence level is extremely high. Our guys thought they were unbeatable.

The game was nationally televised again on ESPN. UCA had won its semifinal game in overtime, adding to the idea that they were this year's "team of destiny." They were playing their best basketball at the end of the season, which of course is what we all want our teams to do. They presented some matchup problems for us, especially with their versatility. Senior forward Joe Sitkowski could score inside and out, and we made the decision to guard him with Keith Stewart, our 6'9 center. But Stewart was less than comfortable defending away from the basket, and UCA exploited the matchup problem. Sitkowski went to the perimeter which took away our rim protection and before we could make a defensive change, he had done some damage from behind the arc. When we put a smaller defender on him, he would move inside and ended the first half with a whopping 21 points. UCA knew us better than anybody and their game plan execution was near perfection. We weren't making shots but still managed a halftime lead of 36-34. We held a slim lead most of the second half but could never pull away. Sitkowski scored a bucket with less than a minute to play which pulled them within two, at 62-60. We turned it over on our next possession and UCA tied the game with 5 seconds remaining. We missed our last attempt in regulation and with the game tied at 62, we were going to overtime. This was our first overtime game of the season, and truthfully, we hadn't played in many close games. UCA had experience on their side when it came to winning in close games. Were they really a team of destiny? One of the great things about sports is you find out what you're made of in pressure situations such as this. Where else can a kid learn so many of life's lessons like dedication, sacrifice, work ethic, teamwork, and sportsmanship? These players were under the most pressure they'd ever known. Here we were in overtime, in front of a national TV audience, with a 53-game winning streak and a national championship on the line. The pressure on these kids was enormous and would be telling. It was the biggest test of their lives. But there was no team I ever had more confidence in, or wanted to go to battle with more than these guys. The next five minutes of overtime would tell the final story.

We had our own strategy going into the overtime period. Sitkowski had been spectacular on the offensive end but had to be careful on defense with four personal fouls. Our game plan was to go at him on every offensive possession to get a bucket or a foul, which the latter would send him to the bench. The strategy worked and only 17 seconds into overtime, Sitkowski was whistled for his fifth foul and was finished for the night, and for the season. We started to pull away and when Smokey drove the lane with just over a minute left, he scored the bucket and was fouled. He completed the three-point play and we led by four points, 73-69. Our guys never looked back and we cruised to an overtime victory with a final score of 82-73. The Chiefs were national champions … Again!

Oklahoma City University Men's Basketball (NAIA) has the longest win streak in men's college basketball in the past 50 years. The 1990-91 and 1991-92 OCU Chiefs won 56 straight games en route to consecutive NAIA National Championships. The 1991 Championship team had a record of 35-3 while the 1992 team had a perfect 38-0 record winning back-to-back national titles. (Wikipedia.org 12-3-24)

I had never been prouder of a team. Most non-sports people fail to understand how difficult it is to win a championship. And it's near impossible to go undefeated, taking every team's best shot every night. To be ranked #1 in the nation from preseason to postseason, was a monumental accomplishment for our players, our fans, and our university. It was the pinnacle of my coaching career and validated my own efforts, my passion, and my dedication. I had no idea that the day of the national championship would be the last game I would ever coach at Oklahoma City University.

"I am the vine, you are the branches. Apart from me you can do nothing." John 5:15

CHAPTER 9 - BAD TO THE BONE

The celebration was on again after winning the title a second time. With the second straight championship and a 54-game winning streak under our belt, it was time to think about the future. We would have some key losses to graduation, but had a solid nucleus back and recruiting was going great. Smokey McCovery was voted the MVP of the national tournament and Eric Manuel was voted first-team all-American. I was named national coach of the year for the second consecutive year, and the fourth straight time in our conference. I've never been much for individual awards in a team sport, but it was flattering to be recognized. Our players were treated like royalty on campus having made school history in such a big way. Most of the guys enjoyed the celebrations and being treated like celebrities. But Eric was different. He never wanted to be the center of attention and seemed almost embarrassed when he received any kind of special treatment. He had no desire for fame or notoriety; he just wanted to play and be a part of the team. In fact, the happiest day for Eric Manuel while at OCU had nothing to do with basketball. The most emotion I ever saw from Eric was the day he walked across the stage of the convention center in downtown Oklahoma City to receive his diploma. After all the criticism and talk about his ACT score, his academic record, and the eligibility questions …. Eric Manuel received his degree from Oklahoma City University. With his mom, Mary, in attendance at commencement, Eric became a college graduate. He was all smiles and tears, and Mary was so very proud of her son. I had delivered on the promises I had made to the Manuel family. With two national championships and his degree in hand, it was a proud day for all of us. Eric was vindicated. He went on to play professional basketball for a while before getting a job and making his home in Oklahoma City. In 1999 Eric Manuel was inducted into the OCU Sports Hall of Fame. His iconic picture hangs in the lobby of the Abe Lemons Center on the OCU campus and rightfully so, has become an OCU legend. And in 2025, Eric was selected for the Macon, Georgia Sports Hall of Fame. No one is more deserving, and no one has fought harder to realize his dreams. I'm so incredibly proud of the man he's become.

The national championships were great for our program, for recruiting, for our university, and for student recruitment and retention. They were obviously good for my resume as well. In 1992 I was looking at my options when the Baylor University head coaching job opened up. They had fired their basketball coach, Gene Iba, who was considered a first-rate basketball coach and a member of the prestigious Iba family. The program at Baylor had suffered through four straight losing seasons, dismal attendance at games, and waning interest due to their lack of competitiveness. I thought Baylor was a sleeping giant in college basketball and the best Division One job opening in the Spring of 1992. They had attracted good enough players in the past, with NBA standouts like Vinnie Johnson, Terry Teagle, and David Wesley. A lot of college coaching jobs are basically already filled before the job even opens. But Baylor's sports administration was in transition. Grant Teaff was a legendary football coach at BU but had resigned to become the athletic director. They also put together a search committee to screen applicants and make recommendations. By now I had become what I thought to be a good recruiter, and I worked hard to get this job, recruiting everyone on the committee. After a couple of weeks of screening, I got the call from the chairman inviting me for an on-campus interview with the committee, and with Coach Teaff. My assistant at OCU, Win Case, had become a hot commodity in the coaching job market and had opportunities as well. He decided to accept an assistant job at St. Louis University with legendary coach Charlie Spoonhour. But I felt certain that if the Baylor job fell in place, I could convince Win to come with me. Win was responsible for most of our recruiting at OCU and really had more to do with the championships than I did. He was the guy that got all these players on our campus. Win is considered one of the best recruiters around, but he's vastly underrated as a coach. He continues to have a stellar career at the Division One level.

During the interview, I spent most of the day with committee members and then met Coach Teaff for dinner. I was a bit intimidated by Teaff. He was a giant in the coaching profession and a living legend at Baylor. But everything went well, and word got out that I was one of three finalists for the job. I was also scheduled to interview with Vice President Jim Netherton at the Final Four in

Minneapolis the following week. The National Association of Basketball Coaches (NABC) convention meets every year at the Final 4. Win was with me in Minneapolis, and he came with me to the interview with Netherton. I thought it was a given that Win would come with me as an assistant, and he would make a great impression on the VP. It was odd that Netherton had been given the task of interviewing coaching candidates, and it became quickly apparent that he had no real idea about basketball, or coaching in general. He was poorly prepared for conducting interviews and really didn't even know what questions to ask. My best shot at getting the job was Teaff and the committee, both of which I felt a strong connection. I was already getting premature calls from coaches who wanted to be on my staff at Baylor. Interestingly, I also got a call from John Macleod, the head coach at Notre Dame. Macleod was pushing his graduate assistant, Steve Hudson, for an assistant position. I knew Steve and liked him a lot but wasn't even certain at this point I was getting the job. But I told Macleod that I would give Steve strong consideration if I did get hired. He said he would call Teaff to recommend me. It's a kind of quid pro quo when it comes to getting a head coaching job in major college sports, much the same as it is in politics I would assume. I got a call the next week from Grant Teaff inviting me back to campus for a second interview. At this point, I figured I might be the front-runner for the job. And sure enough, he offered me the job, I accepted, and we started talking about a contract. What resulted was a five-year deal as head coach at Baylor, making more money than I ever thought possible. It also included revenue from camps, TV and radio shows, endorsements, a shoe contract, a courtesy car, and performance incentives related to success on and off the court. This is the kind of thing that everyone who enters the coaching profession dreams about.

  Before I left for the night, he asked me if I knew all the people who had called him on my behalf. All I knew was that Macleod said he would put in a good word. But Teaff gave me a name that shocked me. He had received a call from the head football coach at Notre Dame, Lou Holtz. Holtz and I had never met, and there's no way he knew me, but said he had watched our championship game on ESPN and was impressed. Obviously, he was calling Teaff at the request of John Macleod, who was trying to get Hudson a job on my staff. The truth was that none of this really mattered in the end but demonstrates how people try and use their influence for personal favors or rewards. To this day, I believe I got the Baylor job on my own record and my own merit, and the favorable impression I had made on Teaff and the search committee. This was a dream come true. Not just being a Division One head basketball coach but being at a program with such potential. Baylor University was the big time … going head-to-head with some of the nation's elite basketball powers. After suffering through four straight losing seasons, it was the perfect job at the perfect time for the new coach. Coach Gene Iba was a part of the most recognizable and elite basketball families in the country. He was the nephew of Oklahoma State and Olympic gold medal coach Henry Iba, the son of longtime coach Clarence Iba, and the cousin of former Nebraska and TCU coach, Moe Iba. It was puzzling why he never got things going at Baylor, because he was a very well-respected coach.

I called Dr. Walker to let him know of my decision to leave OCU. He was somewhat expecting it and handled it in a completely professional manner as I knew he would. I was excited about being one of the 300 major college head coaches in the country. And past the excitement, I was extremely confident that we could do great things at Baylor. My OCU team had a Dunkel power rating as the 51st-best college team in the country, regardless of level. Baylor's rating was 156th, even though they were playing in a whole different stratosphere. But it's an indication of how good our OCU teams were, and how far we had to go at Baylor. My thought was if we can get a power ranking at an NAIA school that's ahead of two-thirds of the division one teams, how hard could it be to improve on four straight losing seasons?

After I accepted the Baylor job, Win resigned at St. Louis, presumably to join me at Baylor. But he also had discussions with Dr. Walker at OCU about becoming the new head coach there. No one deserved the job more than he did, but selfishly I wanted him with me at Baylor. He would have to make the decision based on what was best for his own career. With three job offers on the table, Win felt like he needed head coaching experience more than he needed a major college assistant's job. He accepted the head coaching position at Oklahoma City. I was disappointed to be losing him because we were a team that worked well together. But I respected his opportunity, and Win went on to have great success at OCU and created a legacy of his own. I still consider him one of my closest friends in the coaching profession.

On May 12, 1992, Baylor University held a press conference to introduce me as their new head basketball coach. It was my first time to address the media, fans, staff, and supporters of Baylor University. It was upbeat and full of hopes, dreams, and promise. I had to move forward quickly with hiring a staff. I retained Bryan England from the previous staff in a non-recruiting assistant role. He knew the lay of the land and could help me with making the transition. And he knew the current players and signees better than I did. I had my two full-time assistant positions available and those needed to be filled by experienced recruiters. It seemed my phone was always ringing in those first few weeks after taking the job. Calls from guys looking to join the staff at Baylor, and those who were making recommendations. We interviewed half a dozen candidates before making the selection. I made the decision not to narrow the choices to coaches that I knew personally. I wanted the best coaches I could find, especially in the area of division one recruiting experience. The guy I really wanted I only knew by reputation. Kevin Gray had been an assistant to Wimp Sanderson at Alabama and was respected as maybe the top recruiter in the Southeastern Conference. Wimp had just been let go due to a personal situation in the athletic department, and Kevin wasn't going to get the promotion to head coach. So, he was looking for a job at just the right time as far as I was concerned. He had other offers but eventually decided to join my staff at Baylor. I was super excited about getting such a high-level coach. For the other assistant, I hired Gary Thomas, who had been an assistant for Coach Mike Newell from Lamar University. I became acquainted with Newell when he was an assistant coach for Billy Tubbs at Oklahoma. Mike highly recommended Gary Thomas and I was impressed with his knowledge of the recruiting base in Texas. We were way past the signing period for adding new players, and we had no scholarships left to offer anyway. Coach Iba had touted the incoming players as his best recruiting class ever, but the reality was that they looked pretty average to me. But we would have to play with the cards we were dealt. I recall seeing all of our players working out for the first time and thinking we would be lucky to win a game. My players at OCU were far superior, and we were trying to compete now at a much higher level. It would likely be a very long season.

With recruiting out of the way I was charged with trying to

generate some interest and enthusiasm in our program that had been sorely lacking. The consensus of the Baylor administration and supporters was that Gene Iba was a good enough coach, but that the talent level was not where it needed to be. In addition, Gene was an old-school X's and O's type who didn't feel a need to market the program or worry about attendance at games. The Iba style of basketball was more of a slowed-down offense, with an overriding emphasis on defense. It was a solid strategy, but it wasn't a modern style of play or one that fans found endearing and was even less attractive to prospective players.

So, I dedicated the entire summer to promoting a new era of Baylor basketball. We would be wide-open and up-tempo on offense while trying to create offense through a pressure-type defense. The media even nicknamed us "the running Bears," before we ever played a game. I took every speaking engagement, spoke to every civic club, joined two different country clubs and did nothing else but try and create excitement about a new brand of basketball in town. And it was working. I became immensely popular in the Waco community mostly because I was just a regular guy who happened to be a basketball coach and was passionate about bringing success to this program. The message was resonating and contagious. There was excitement in the air, and people were all of a sudden buying season tickets. Now I knew we might have a lousy season, but I was determined to get the most out of what we had, and to at least be entertaining. Baylor had just built a new facility for its basketball teams, and other special events. The capacity for the Ferrell Center topped out at around 10,000 but the average attendance for last season had dropped below 3,000. It's difficult to have any type of home-court advantage if no one is coming to your games. So, we had to change that.

We put the players through a rigorous preseason and weight training program before official practices could begin on October 15th, by NCAA rules. Many elite basketball programs hold their first practice at midnight on October 15th to get a jump start and to create an event that would bring excitement for the upcoming season. Baylor had not done so because they feared no one would come. But we decided to hold our first ever "Midnight Madness" official practice of the season. We had a dunk contest, handed out t-shirts, had food and drink available and made it the social event of the year with over 6,000 fans showing up. We hadn't played a game yet, but the town was crazy excited about Baylor basketball.

Since school began in August, we had been relentless in our recruiting efforts. If we didn't improve our talent level, it would be more of the same with losing seasons and a disgruntled fan base. We needed immediate help, so we focused on older players with experience, primarily from the junior college ranks. The early signing period was in November, and we wanted to try and wrap most of it up by then. Our first signees were two players from Westark Junior College in Arkansas. Marcus Thompson was a three-point shooting specialist, while Jerome Lambert had proven to be an elite rebounder. Gary Thomas took the lead in recruiting the Westark players and was getting help from the coaching staff there. Doc Sadler and Troy Drummond were acquainted with Thomas and what is often the case, both were looking for jobs on the coattails of the two players. We also targeted a duo from State Fair Junior College in Sedalia, Missouri. Kevin Gray was most involved in the recruitment of 6'8 Tyrone Davis and point guard Jason Ervin. Both had come to Baylor on official recruiting visits as defined by the NCAA and loved our situation. Both gave us a verbal commitment while on the visit, which is a step in the process but is also non-binding. Both wanted to sign during the November signing period, but their coach at State Fair, Billy Barton, was not going to allow it. Division One coaches often stash high school players in junior college who don't qualify academically for an NCAA scholarship out of high school. The hopes are to create goodwill with the junior college coach and then get them back after they receive a two-year associate's degree from the school. Barton didn't want his players signing early, most likely so he could dangle them in front of major college coaches in the spring, hoping to get a player or two in return. There's no certainty that's what was going on here, but it routinely happens, and no one really talks about it. Again, it's one of those quid pro quo situations. The bottom line was that Davis and Ervin both wanted to sign early with Baylor. We had to make a decision. We could either honor their coach's wish to wait till the Spring which would leave the recruitment process open and take a chance on losing them to another school. Or we could sign them in the early period and not make any public announcement. The National Letter of Intent was binding by NCAA rules, so if we signed them to the NLI, they were bound to Baylor. I decided to run this by my boss, Grant Teaff. Coach Teaff had been a highly successful football coach at BU and knew how important recruiting was, and also how difficult it is to raise your talent level. Plus, he had hired me and wanted us to do well. I could see how signing the State Fair players might be viewed as questionable or even unethical if we did it without telling their coach. On the other hand, Barton didn't appear to have the best interest of the players at heart and was the only obstacle to the two players becoming a part of our program. I trusted Teaff completely. He was not just a great coach, but also a man of faith that I wanted to emulate. Teaff was mostly non-committal and left it up to us. I got the feeling that he wouldn't have done it, but he left the door open for us to go ahead with signing the two Star Fair recruits if that's what we wanted to do. We signed Davis and Ervin to letters of intent and made no announcement. At the players' request, we also did not disclose the fact they had signed with Coach Billy Barton. It was definitely a gray area and maybe a bit sketchy, but we were on a mission and hadn't broken any NCAA rules. In addition to the four junior college guys from out of state, we also signed local products Shannon Brantley from McClennan Junior College in Waco, and high schooler Jerode Banks from Temple, about 30 minutes down the road. I had a history with Coach Ken Deweese at McClennan dating back to my days at Oklahoma Baptist University, which helped us with Brantley. But he was a long shot to qualify academically and had a lot of classroom work to do before becoming Baylor eligible. Banks was a high school All-American at Temple who wanted to remain close to home. Our first recruiting class was stellar, and after the spring semester, were ranked in the top 10 nationally. Even if our season turned out to be a complete bust, we knew the cavalry was coming. But the honeymoon was over, and it was almost time to show and tell.

Our players were pumped about all the excitement generated in the community, and also with the new style of play. The up-tempo game was not just for entertainment purposes, I also thought it was our best chance to win games with the team we had. We were more athletic than I had first thought, and sophomore Aundre Branch had the makings of a star. He hadn't played much as a freshman, but he was our best shooter. We were good enough inside with 6'9 Alex "Chief" Holcomb who was playing in his senior season. We surrounded these guys with mostly role players, but they were solid. Our first game was against Division 3 Hardin-Simmons which should have been an automatic win. We broke open the game after halftime and went on to a convincing 97-64 win, my first at Baylor and as a Division One head coach. At the press conference after the game, I commented that at least we weren't going to be winless. It was my feeble attempt to lower expectations, but I knew this team was not going to be competing at a high level. The best thing about our opening game victory had been the presence of a mentor and friend. Paul Hansen, my boss at Oklahoma State and the guy I learned the most from had come for a visit and was in the stands for my first game as a major college head coach. Paul had recently retired from coaching and was having some health issues but made the long drive just to support his friend. It meant the world to me, but I had no idea it would be the last time I'd ever see him. Paul passed away a couple of months later and the family asked me to deliver the eulogy at his funeral. It was an emotional time as I spoke of what this man had meant to me, to the state of Oklahoma, and to the game of basketball. I truly loved this man like no other. He represented everything that was good in college sports and was like a father to me. What a huge loss. He was only 63 years old.

We managed to win our next three games against average competition, before losing a road game to Oklahoma State and Coach Eddie Sutton, 93-75. It was my first loss as a head coach after 58 consecutive wins. We then won four out of our next five games before starting conference play against TCU and Coach Moe Iba, a game that we won big, 79-57. Our next game would be on the road against the preseason favorite Texas Longhorns. Our guys were playing a little over their heads and with great confidence. They seemed to thrive in the new system, but I was not delusional about our chances of making any post-season noise. In what was likely our best game of the season we beat Texas on the road by a point, 87-86. Fans were coming to games in throngs, and we would actually lead the nation in increased game attendance before the year was over. I became wildly popular in the community, to the point where I had my own theme song played before every home game. "Bad to the Bone" would play when I entered the court area prior to each game. It had been Kevin Gray's idea after Wimp Sanderson had the same song played at Alabama when he came out to the court before each game. One of the editorials in the local Waco newspaper read "Darrel Johnson for Mayor!" It was all a bit silly but to say we had it going was an understatement. We had just beat Texas on the road, crowds were overflowing, and it looked probable that we would at least have a winning season in our first year. And this was with the team that was left to us after four straight losing seasons, and a ranked recruiting class on the horizon. I had my own TV show on a local network and a couple of on-site radio call-in shows. Our summer basketball camps were already filling up and the money coming in was like I never thought possible. We finished the season with a 7-7 league record and 16-11 overall. There were no post-season bids coming our way but that was fine. The season had gone better than expected and the fan base was excited about what we were building. We had a strong nucleus coming back next year to go along with a recruiting class of guys with pro-level potential. The future looked bright ... but things began to unravel pretty quickly.

"In the world you will have tribulation, but be of good cheer. I have overcome the world." John 16:33

CHAPTER 10 - THE BOYCOTT

Denna had settled in being a mom to Derek and was also working towards a master's degree at Baylor. She was supportive in everything I tried to do, was a fantastic mother to our son, and was a devoted coach's wife. We attended church together most Sundays but looking back, my faith was not a priority. Here I was at the largest Baptist University in the world, and having been mostly raised in the Baptist church, felt right at home. In what could have been a great platform for sharing my faith and living a Godly example for others, the faith part of my life was just incidental. The career was front and center and providing for the family was in a distant second place. Denna didn't have to work, and we had plenty of money and means. Her faith was strong, and she was a great ambassador and role model for young women. There were times when I was too busy to notice with an all-encompassing passion for the job, the career, and building this program at Baylor. Denna deserved so much better from me, and it remains one of the great failures of my life.

The 1992-93 basketball season had been cause for celebration. But it was the tip of the iceberg with what we could be in the 93-94 season, with the group of players we had returning combined with our first recruiting class. We had only two scholarships available for the fall signing period in November of 1993 and knew who we wanted. We had signed high school All-American Jerod Banks from Temple High School who was now in his freshman year at Baylor. He had two high school teammates who became our primary targets for the fall signing period. Roderick Miller was a combo guard who we felt was a couple of years away from being a contributor. But we had time for him to be in a backup role playing behind the junior college players we had signed. Roderick's dad, Harry Miller, was also the head coach at Temple and we had developed a solid relationship with him in our previous year while recruiting his senior All-American, Jerode Banks. But the guy we were most excited about was the other player from Temple, 6'10 center Brian Skinner.

Skinner was an athletic big man that we felt certain would become a top NBA prospect. We focused most all of our attention on these two and both signed with us in November. Miller would likely be a guy for the future, but Skinner would be an impact player as a freshman. So, we had wrapped up recruiting in the early signing period and had no more roster spots open. Coach Barton at State Fair filed a formal complaint with the NCAA when he found out his players had signed in November without telling anyone. But we didn't break any rules, despite it being a bad look for our staff, and likely raised an eyebrow with the NCAA enforcement staff. All four of our junior college signees had come to Waco for the summer, and they all needed hours to complete their associate's degree.

NCAA rules prohibited the players from being on scholarship in the summer, and before they were formally eligible to play. So, the players were on their own as far as living expenses and paying for school. We could, however, arrange employment or a summer job for them so they would have some income. NCAA rules were grossly unfair to the student-athletes themselves. They would not be allowed to work during the regular school year or receive any kind of financial supplement to their athletic scholarship. Major college sports generate millions of dollars for the university from donations, gate receipts, television and radio contracts, ticket sales, concessions, advertising and other sources. The players were not entitled to any of that and were not even allowed to have a job to support themselves or their family members. The only thing we could do to help them in the off-season was to help them find a summer job. The job had to be legitimate and in line with what normal compensation might be for the performance of the job. Our four junior college players all came from lower-income family environments and received little financial support from home. So, we had a big task on our hands. The players needed hours to graduate from their respective junior colleges, but even with a job, could not afford private school tuition, especially as expensive as Baylor was. Nor would they be able to attend classes during the day since they all held 8 to 5 jobs, Monday through Friday. This was well before the introduction of the internet or anything like online classes that are offered today. They were all capable students, just needed a few hours of summer school to get fully certified. NCAA rules made it harder than it should have been, and they have changed their rules drastically over the past few years. With the introduction of the NIL (name, image, and likeness) into college sports, players now have an opportunity to get a piece of the NCAA pie. They didn't change willingly, and some are still fighting it. It's taken litigation through the court system to facilitate the changes in favor of the student-athletes.

The only realistic option for our four players was to enroll in correspondence classes or independent study. We had heard about a school in Florida that a lot of the Division One schools were using for correspondence class credits, to help players gain their eligibility status. The Southeastern College of Assembly of God in Lakeland, Florida offered general studies classes that could be taken through correspondence, without the requirement of physical class attendance. As many as 200 colleges and universities had used the SECAG correspondence program to gain credits for student-athletes. The players would have to pay for the courses but were able to do so with their earnings from their summer employment. Southeastern would either send assignments through the mail or via fax to the students, and upon completion, would take exams proctored by any person with a teaching certificate and a college degree. So, during the summer of 1993, our four junior college signees would work during the days and would play pickup games or work out at night. By NCAA rules we weren't allowed to conduct any workouts or even watch pickup games during the off-season. This too, has changed recently, with a relaxing of some of the archaic rules that were in place back then. Coaches can now conduct summer workouts, and even schedule summer team events and trips with their players, as well as arrange for tuition to be paid for summer or online classes.

Our players enrolled in correspondence classes at Southeastern and paid for the classes themselves. We did not want any appearance of being overly involved, so no one on the basketball staff would serve as a proctor for exams, and we documented all payments from the players to the school in Florida. At the end of the summer, all players were NCAA eligible and certified by the Baylor compliance office, the Conference office, and the NCAA. It had been a long road through the summer, but now we were ready to start school with what promised to be a much better team, and maybe a contender.

The women's basketball program at BU had been in turmoil. The coach had been fired in May 1993 and then upon appeal, was reinstated. I never really understood what was going on or the reason behind her dismissal. They had been losing but that's not the reason the Baylor administration gave for firing her. There was something about rules violations, but that seemed to be bogus and was just a way to get rid of her after eight straight losing seasons. The press release said something to the effect that "she was not operating her program properly." (Sports Illustrated, Nov 28, 1994). In any event, she was now back coaching her team. But on August 30th, we got word that she had sent a memo to the Baylor administration documenting possible rules violations by the men's basketball program. Grant Teaff had resigned to become the director of the American Football Coaches Association and was replaced by his assistant, Dick Ellis. The memo alleging 10 violations mostly contained what the NCAA would consider secondary or minor violations, but it also called into question the eligibility of our four junior college players. It was definitely a cloud over our program and eventually got the attention of the media and the NCAA. There were rumors circulating that the NCAA was investigating our program, which would of course hinder our further recruiting efforts. But all we could do was get ready for our season, which looked promising. Our new guys were dominating in practice, and our talent level was much improved. The chemistry seemed good, we had no big weaknesses, and we were deep. Ervin and Thompson were big-time shooters and would thrive along with returnee Aundre Branch. Davis was a bit undersized for the center position at 6'8 but played bigger. Brantley was our best athlete, and Lambert was a dominating rebounder, reminiscent of Dennis Rodman. Everything was going according to plan except this NCAA cloud wouldn't go away, and it had enough traction to attract media attention from all over the country. We just wanted to get the season going and start winning games. The day before our first exhibition game, I got a call from Dick Ellis, our new athletic director. He asked me to come meet with him about an urgent matter. Urgent is rarely a positive thing so of course I became nervous. When I got to his office it was obvious that we had a problem. As I sat down and braced myself, he began speaking. He told me that the University, in conjunction with the conference leadership, had decided to withhold our four junior college players from competition until further notice. He said it was likely that the NCAA would be involved, and leadership did not want to take the chance that we might have certified players that the NCAA could subsequently decide were not eligible to participate. He specifically named our President, Dr. Herb Reynolds, as the one who had signed off on it. I had lots of questions, most notably "for how long." The "suspension" as I called it, was for an indefinite length of time according to Ellis. I left the office after the short meeting, completely unaware of how in the world I was going to tell my players. They had been certified as eligible by the university, the league's compliance, and the NCAA clearinghouse. They had worked their tails off all summer and fall to be eligible to play, and we were all excited about the prospects for a hugely successful season. When I got back to the arena before practice, I called the four into my office and gave them the news. The players had trusted me and the university process. They wanted to know why this was happening and I had no real reason to offer. It was the day before the first game, and we would have four starters sitting on the bench in street clothes. As a college coach, I cannot begin to describe how important it is to establish a trust and bond between coach and players. They felt like we had failed them after they had put their trust in us. I had to do something to let them know we were all in this together and committed to a positive resolution. And I did. I put out a press release the day of the first game through our sports information office.

"I will not be in attendance at tonight's game in support of the four players who are not being allowed to participate. Each of these players has been certified as eligible by Baylor University and Southwest Conference compliance, as well as the NCAA clearinghouse. It is my belief that these players have completed all necessary scholastic requirements that would allow full participation as student-athletes at Baylor. It is my fervent hope that this process, whatever it may be, can come to a quick resolution to get these four young men back on the basketball court." Darrel Johnson, Head Basketball Coach – Baylor University

It was a bold move that endeared me with the players and most Baylor fans, but didn't sit well with the school's administration. It's amazing that most college administrators actually seem to know very little about intercollegiate athletics. To me, it was like no one at the university cared about these kids, whose life's passion was competing on the basketball court. The most important thing to the BU administration appeared to be falling in line with the NCAA, rather than supporting the program or these kids. There are also countless examples of strong college presidents, athletic directors, and others who stood up to the NCAA enforcement staff and infractions committee, only to have penalties reduced or eliminated. But the BU president was not happy and sent me a message to get back on the court for the next game. They were calling it a boycott, but my only real purpose was to support my players. My next press release stated the obvious, that it was my job to coach and support ALL of my players, and that I would be back on the bench for the next game. We had a job to do, even if it was putting a team on the floor that would not be nearly as competitive as it would have been with our full roster.

The regular season started with only seven scholarship players eligible to participate. Team morale should have been dismally low, but our seven guys were excited. We did have one of our junior college players who was allowed to play, and he was a dandy. Jerome Lambert from Westark Community College was one of our top priorities in recruiting for the 1993-94 season. His teammate at Westark, Marcus Thompson, was one of the four who were sitting out. We were never sure why Jerome was singled out among the others, but we were glad to have him. He was a monster rebounder and gave us a legitimate inside presence at the power-forward spot. Outside of Lambert, we were basically putting the same team on the floor as we had the previous year, but with much less depth and bench. Crowds were as good as they had been the previous year, and we responded by winning seven of our first eight games. Our only loss was on the road to a ranked Arizona team, where my brother Phil was an assistant coach. They went on to win a national championship while Phil was there, and they thumped us pretty good in Tucson. Lambert was leading the nation in rebounding and Aundre Branch was shooting the lights out from the perimeter. Branch was the best shooter in the league with unlimited range and high-level athleticism. We had planned to redshirt freshman Jerode Banks but now he was a starter, and showing promise as a potential star down the road. Doug Brandt, a 6'10 redshirt freshman started at the center position, was solid on both ends, and was destined to have a productive career at Baylor. Nelson Haggerty was returning as our point guard, and Willie Sublett was back at the small forward position. It was not a team that would contend for championships, but we hoped to have our other four guys back into the rotation soon. And when that happened, we would potentially be an NCAA tournament team that could go deep into the postseason. But the investigation into our program continued, and even though they were allowed to practice with the team, Shannon Brantley, Marcus Thompson, Jason Ervin, and Tyrone Davis never suited up for a single game. The season had its ups and downs and considering the circumstances, and having only seven scholarship players, most would call it a successful year. In truth, the team we faced in practice every day was better than the team we put on the floor in games. We finished the season with an identical record from the previous year at 16-11 overall, and 7-7 in league play. It was our second straight winning season, but there was no postseason, and we were left with the difficult thought of what might have been. It was a major disappointment to the coaches and players, who knew we had final four potential with our full complement of players. Instead, we lost in the first round of the conference tournament and our season ended abruptly. It would be a tumultuous off-season and summer for Baylor basketball.

·

"My conscience is clear, but that does not make me innocent. It is the Lord who judges me." 1 Corinthians 4:4

CHAPTER 11 - THE INVESTIGATION

Our recruiting for the next year was hamstrung because we went through the April 1994 signing period not knowing the ultimate fate of our four junior college players who had been forced to the sidelines last season. The investigation had been handed over to an independent law firm which was headed by former NCAA enforcement officer, Mike Glazier. Glazier had found a lucrative niche in private practice investigating sports programs for rules violations. Typically, he was hired by the school itself but also could be employed by a specific conference entity or NCAA affiliate. It was thought that with his background as an NCAA investigator, he might better understand the enforcement process and could even mitigate potential NCAA penalties for rules infractions. It was also believed by many that Glazier was still cozy with current NCAA investigators and might have access to inside information pertaining to ongoing investigations. But most NCAA coaches became fearful of his involvement in their programs, because he typically represented the conference or the university, and not the individual coaches. He was basically a hired gun to dig up dirt on coaches and rule breakers, who would then end up as collateral damage.

In cases of NCAA rules violations, there are varying thoughts as to who should be held most responsible. It might be the coaching staff, the boosters, the athletic administration, the sports compliance office, or even the student athletes themselves. It can be a tricky and complicated question but apparently, Glazier went straight for the coaching staff, whom he considered to be most expendable. The success of his thriving business model was not dependent on coaches liking him, but rather on having satisfied the expectations of his paying customers … the schools themselves. He was careful not to alienate university or conference administration, often at the expense of coaches. Baylor University has had more than its fair share of NCAA problems which is well documented. While it's been the coaches themselves that have ended up taking the fall in most cases, Baylor's compliance office during my tenure was laughable. The department was comprised of two track coaches at the University, which represented an obvious potential for conflict of interest, not to mention a lack of real training or understanding of complex NCAA rules and interpretations. They seemed to be perfectly aligned with Glazier and his firm in the investigation of our program. But it's also important to note that not everyone was a fan of Mike Glazier.

Former Pitt football coach and ESPN analyst Mike Gottfried says, *"Glazier does a horrible job. If Glazier says it, then the NCAA concludes it happened. Nobody oversees him. He's like a bounty hunter." Steve Beckett, the lawyer for former Illinois basketball star Deon Thomas, agrees with Gottfried. Though they were never proved, allegations that Thomas had been offered improper inducements when he was being recruited by Illinois led the school to hire Glazier in 1990. "Glazier sells coaches down the river to make schools look good," Beckett says. "If your school wants to work within the good-ol'-boy system and doesn't care about its coaches and players, hire him. One reason colleges hire Glazier is because of his relationship with the NCAA, where he worked for seven years as an investigator. His ninth-floor office in Overland Park commands a view of NCAA headquarters half a mile away. He used to play lunch-hour basketball with NCAA enforcement chief David Berst, and they still play golf together. Chuck Smrt, an NCAA enforcement director, was Glazier's roommate for a year when both were undergraduates at Indiana and Glazier's former partner, Mike Slive, is now the chairman of the NCAA infractions appeals committee. Smrt declined to discuss Glazier, and Slive had no comment on any possible conflict of interest."* Beckett says *"He takes a cookie-cutter approach, you fire the coach, get rid of the player, admit you did all these things but say you've got institutional control because you cleaned house, and beg for mercy from the NCAA. Then Glazier and his people get satisfied clients by convincing them they would have lost it all without them."* (Sports Illustrated, May 23, 1994).

The conflicts of interest go way beyond those described in the Sports Illustrated article referenced. For example, a former Villanova athletic director, Vince Icastro, hired Glazier to investigate their program, then later became a member of the NCAA's Committee on Infractions. Mike Slive, former business partner of Glazier and SEC commissioner, later became the chairman of the NCAA's Infractions

Appeals Committee. There are numerous other examples of improper associations and lack of due process. But what is perhaps the "smoking gun" of conflict of interest, Glazier's roommate at the University of Indiana, Chuck Smrt, worked as an NCAA investigator and was one of those involved with the Eric Manuel case at Kentucky. That would be the same Eric Manuel who played on two national championship teams at Oklahoma City University for Darrel Johnson, now the Baylor coach. There are those who smell a conspiracy here. Eric Manuel is banned for life from the NCAA after an investigation by Chuck Smrt and others of the NCAA. Manuel then sues, and wins, for the right to play at OCU and leads his team to 54 straight wins. Now the NCAA is investigating Baylor basketball where Manuel's former OCU coach is now the head coach. And the lead investigator for the Baylor investigation is Mike Glazier, Smrt's old college buddy and roommate. It may be challenging to follow the proverbial bouncing ball, but this sure looks fishy. Maybe it's just a coincidence. But the investigation continues through the spring and summer at a snail's pace, while billable hours are piling up for Glazier and his firm.

Shortly after the completion of the 1993-94 season, BU women's coach Pam Bowers was fired again. This time the reason given was the result of another losing season. She had made internal allegations to Baylor's administration about possible rules violations committed by the men's basketball program, and she alleged that was the reason she was fired. She also had complained about the disparity between budget allocations and salaries for the men's and women's programs at Baylor and claimed she had been a victim of sex discrimination and wrongful termination. She later testified with compliance personnel associated with the university, the Southwest Conference and the NCAA, and also filed a multi-million-dollar lawsuit against the university. Also named in her lawsuit were BU administrators Grant Teaff, Dick Ellis, Clyde Hart, and James Netherton. The individual defendants were eventually removed from the lawsuit by the Court, and the case was settled out of court for an undisclosed amount of money awarded to Bowers. She was done at Baylor but did not go quietly and created enough havoc at the institution to last for many years. I was left in a position of fighting for our program but not really knowing what had caused the NCAA to investigate. Bowers was labeled in the media as a whistleblower and that certainly could have been a reason. But after all these years

I am more inclined to lean towards the retribution of the NCAA as the reason behind the scrutiny of our program. Or maybe it was both … or even something entirely different. We will likely never know.

During the summer of 1994, still with no resolution, our players started transferring to other schools. Tyrone Davis left for Kansas State and Jerome Lambert transferred to Oklahoma State with only one year of eligibility remaining. Marcus Thompson ended up at Murray State and Jason Ervin at Central Oklahoma. No one expected them to stay at Baylor with all that was happening and with the unresolved eligibility issues. It was in the Spring of 1994 that I was offered a golden parachute and a way out of this mess at Baylor. I had another job offer. The Oklahoma City Cavalry of the Continental Basketball Association (CBA) asked me to be their new head coach, after the dismissal of former coach Henry Bibby. The CBA was the developmental league for the NBA and might be a steppingstone to a new career in professional basketball. A major draw for our family was that it was back home, in Oklahoma. Ownership of the team was led by Chip Land, who I knew casually. Chip saw marketing potential with a coach who had Oklahoma roots and had won championships in the same market. The downside was that I had no experience coaching on the pro side of basketball and it was entirely a different animal. But he saw what we had done with game attendance in Waco and the Cavs needed a boost in ticket sales, with a home-grown head coach. It was flattering, timely, and extremely tempting. The compensation was smaller than what I had at Baylor but was loaded with incentives that could equal or even surpass the package at Baylor if we were successful. The word had leaked out to the press that I'd received this job offer and most people expected me to accept given the current circumstances. I decided I needed to take this to the big boss on campus, Dr. Herb Reynolds, Baylor's President.

The meeting with Reynolds was anything but cordial. He didn't like the predicament we were in, and it was obvious that he blamed me. Plus, he didn't like the fact that I had skipped a game in protest to support the suspended players. Reynolds was the consummate academician who appeared to lack any deep understanding of the inner workings of intercollegiate athletics. But he wanted us to win, not to embarrass the university, and of course, I feel certain he liked the money that the major sports, football and basketball, brought to the institution. That seemed to me to be the top level of his interest in major college scholastic competition. He never asked about the kids in our program or about anything specific pertaining to the team. I explained to him the decision that I had been presented with and was looking for advice. Taking the Cavalry job was a way out for me and maybe my exit could actually help the situation at Baylor. It had become apparent that I was the primary target of the investigation being conducted by the league, and on behalf of the NCAA. There were others who felt the NCAA inquiry was more of a vendetta against me in retaliation for the Eric Manuel victory. The Baylor investigation was being documented on a daily basis in the national media, and if you followed college sports, you knew what was going on. My former boss and President of Oklahoma City University, Dr. Jerald Walker was following as well and had written a personal letter to Reynolds. His letter dated April 7, 1994, read in part …

"Coach Johnson's tenure at OCU was consistently marked by the very highest levels of integrity and character. He was a coach who was genuinely concerned with winning games as his championships attest, but also with the academic and overall development of student-athletes. He always represented the university in an exemplary manner. He also showed a strong commitment to academic integrity and adherence to University and intercollegiate regulations, policies, and procedures. I find it reprehensible and offensive that his character and conduct are in question. I detect a possible undercurrent of vindictiveness and scapegoatism of the NCAA's hounding of Eric Manuel. I find this possibility thoroughly repugnant. Mr. Manuel graduated on time and was a sound student while at OCU. He won his court case due to sloppy administrative action on the part of NAIA officials. There is reason to believe that influence from NCAA officials helped the NAIA choose its ill-considered course of action. If I may provide additional information, please let me know." Jerald C. Walker – President, Oklahoma City University

Wow! Walker was in his usual championship form! Reynolds acknowledged he had received the letter from Walker in our meeting but made no mention of its content. It was later that another OCU administrator had forwarded a copy to me, which I still have in my possession today.

I explained to Reynolds my thoughts on both sides of the decision I had to make but stated that it was my desire to remain at Baylor. I put my decision squarely on Reynolds' shoulders stating quite clearly that my first consideration was protecting and providing for my family. I bluntly told him, "If you're going to fire me over this I need to know now. I have an opportunity to extend my career and continue taking care of my wife and son. If you're planning to fire me, or if it will help the cause, I will go quietly. But I just need to know ... now."

Reynolds looked stunned that I would be so candid with him. But things did not look good at this point, and we had no way of getting better in the short term since we were not able to replace the four players who were leaving the program. Reynolds was measured in his reply to the question put before him. He thought for a minute and then chose to answer with a non-answer. He said if I had a clear conscience about the allegations and accusations related to our program, then I should follow my conscience. To me, that was telling me to stay. I left the meeting telling him I would be in touch. There was a lot to think about and yes, to pray about. This was a decision that would chart the course of my career.

The next month was spent talking, thinking, and praying over my decision. Basketball was in its off-season and Cavalry owner Chip Land had no sense of urgency for me to decide my next move. There was no apparent movement in terms of the investigation during this time either. Most of my true friends were advising me to leave, while most Baylor fans wanted me to stay. A Baylor booster had come forward and had given Denna and me a Caribbean cruise as an incentive to stay. We left for the Caribbean to get away from all the drama and pressure, and to talk about what to do next. We did sign a couple of high school players after the April signing period, but we did not expect either to be able to help us immediately. The top talent in this year's recruiting class had all signed early and elsewhere. On June 6, 1994, I issued the following press release through the Baylor Sports Information Office...

"I have declined the generous job offer from the Oklahoma City Cavalry of the Continental Basketball Association. I have the highest respect and admiration for owner Chip Land and the entire Cavalry organization. However, I came to Baylor two years ago intending to remain here for the rest of my career. I signed a five-

year contract and, at the least, intend to fulfill the commitment I made to Baylor. While I cannot comment specifically on the investigation of our program, I have a clear conscience regarding my personal involvement in the alleged infractions. I have never knowingly, willfully or intentionally violated NCAA or conference rules. Although I do not know the specifics of Michael Glazier's report (Glazier is the special investigator reporting to the conference), nor do I know what action may be taken by the NCAA, I believe that we can work through whatever penalties may be imposed."

Most everyone was surprised by the decision. It was a respectful way out of an impossible situation at Baylor. But it also would have ended my dream as a major college coach, and I would obviously be leaving the program in a huge mess. Not to mention the bad optics it would present, and the appearance I had "cut and run." I didn't want to leave and felt a responsibility to clean things up and get the Baylor program back on track. Chip Land was most gracious in his own press release,

"I knew Darrel was feeling a very strong obligation to the university, and it might very well be moralistically the right thing for him to do - to stay there and defend his reputation. He's a great coach and friend, and I wish him the best." Chip Land, Owner – Oklahoma City Cavalry

The decision was made, and we needed to make the most of what we had. We now needed to concentrate on the NCAA matters before us. It was apparent that we were in over our heads and needed counsel. Me and my assistant coaches, Kevin Gray, Gary Thomas, and Troy Drummond all retained a local attorney, David Cherry, to represent us in the investigation. He advised us that we all needed to stay on the same page and coached us through our individual interviews with Mike Glazier. We all gave our statements and answered questions from Glazier about our program. Shortly thereafter, the Southwest Conference, represented by Glazier's firm, issued a 544-page report alleging 28 rules infractions against the men's basketball program. Many were considered secondary violations but the most damaging were accusations of what they called "academic fraud" and accused our coaching staff, and others, of improperly helping our junior college recruits gain their eligibility through correspondence courses. After consultations with the Baylor administration about the report, Cherry called a meeting with all the coaches.

The mood was serious, and the evidence was damning. Cherry said that based on his conversations with the BU brass, the three assistant coaches had no chance of keeping their jobs. He also said that I was the only one with a chance to survive this and advised the assistant coaches to resign their positions before being fired by Baylor. They agreed and resigned, while I promised to do everything I could to help them get other jobs. Gray was looking for a high school coaching job back in his home state of Kentucky and Thomas wanted to be back in Kansas where he had previously coached. I made numerous calls for both of them trying to help, but the publicity surrounding our program took away most of the influence I might have otherwise had. Thomas landed a high school job in Kansas and Gray eventually ended up coaching at Spalding University. Drummond had a solid career at Howard Payne University in Texas.

Baylor would not allow me to hire a full staff, anticipating sanctions that could be levied from the NCAA. But I did hire one coach … Harry Miller from Temple High School. Harry and I had developed a good relationship while recruiting his players, and I admired his coaching style, as well as his character and faith. Harry accepted and, at Baylor, he would be coaching three of his former players at Temple, including his own son. I had to continue the fight to save my job while at the same time preparing for another season. We had lost our best players, but we were not void of talent. Aundre Branch was back and had been our leading scorer for the past two years. Point guard Nelson Haggerty returned as did our 6'10 center, Doug Brandt. Jerode Banks had the most potential of any returnee and had averaged in double figures as a freshman. Plus we had a couple of other solid role players, as well as one of the best freshmen in the country in 6'10 center Brian Skinner. I convinced myself we could still win, at least to the extent we had won the past two years. But the publicity surrounding our program continued to worsen, and we were the subject of designated stories on network news shows, ESPN, Sports Illustrated and virtually every major news outlet in America. We were getting no support from the university administration as almost everyone was doing everything they could to try and distance themselves from me, the basketball program, and the ongoing controversy. Even those in the coaching fraternity whom I considered friends bailed out and cut ties. Harry and I got along great, but I was in this fight by myself, though still retaining my attorney, David Cherry. I thought if we could get through the summer, get school started and begin the season then maybe everything would work out. The BU community was still mostly supportive, but I could feel the pendulum swinging in the wrong direction. We needed something positive to happen. I left town on vacation the week before school started. It was a time to reflect, do some soul-searching, and prepare myself mentally for the upcoming year. I was in Lake Tahoe, Nevada when I got the phone call that changed everything. Jerode Banks, our most talented returning player and the brightest hope for the future of Baylor basketball was dead.

"We also glory in our sufferings, because we know that suffering produces perseverance, character, and hope." Romans 5:3

CHAPTER 12 – INDICTED

Jerode Banks was killed in a one-car collision on the interstate in an early morning crash on August 25, 1994. Speculation was that he fell asleep at the wheel driving in between Waco and Temple, after running into an overpass support on Interstate 35. The ensuing fire burned the body past recognition and was later identified through dental records. Jerode "Smokey" Banks was gone. I caught the first plane I could get out of Nevada back to Waco. This was a tragic loss for his teammates and coaches, but even more so for his family and close friends. Upon my return, I met with the family who were obviously grief-stricken and beyond devastated. There was nothing I could do or say that would ease their pain, but we prayed together in his Temple home. Coach Miller was even closer to Jerode and his family than I was, having coached him in high school. Miller was overcome with grief and sadness. The loss of a potential superstar for our basketball team paled in comparison to the family's loss. I could not imagine a parent having to endure such pain. A few days later, I delivered the eulogy at Jerode's funeral in Temple. Banks was a phenom athlete and a great kid, but I didn't really know much about his faith walk. I knew he came from a Christian home and talked about it at the funeral. I ended the eulogy talking about Jerode's athleticism and ability to play above the rim. But now, I said, "We can be assured that Jerode "Smokey" Banks was in a very special place, that was way, way above the rim." They call it a celebration of life, but it was an unbelievably sad day for all of us who knew him.

The tragedy of losing Banks was incredibly hard for our team. He was emerging as a leader and a player we had come to count on. His attitude and work ethic were over the top. His skill set and athleticism was among the nation's elite, and we could not be the same team without him. But we had to move forward.

We started the fall semester and preseason workouts with the team. We still had good players, but our overall talent level and depth had taken a major hit with the loss of Jerode and our four junior college recruits. The juco kids had all transferred and became eligible to play at other schools. We started official practices on October 15th, which was the first date allowed by NCAA rules. We thought about Jerode every single day but knew he would want us all to compete to the best of our ability. We practiced hard and prepared for the upcoming season. Our first exhibition game was scheduled for November 19th, with the regular season slated to begin on November 27th. We're concentrating on the upcoming season but the investigation into our program is still ongoing. Only now we're hearing rumors that the United States Attorney's office might be involved in our case. My attorney, David Cherry, thinks there's something up with the Feds taking an interest in the investigation. Cherry doesn't think I'm a potential target but believes that my three former assistants might be. For the first time ever, we're beginning to hear things like "wire fraud" and "mail fraud" being thrown around in reference to the NCAA investigation of our program. I'm in total disbelief that this could even be a remote possibility. It was, however, becoming clear that the NCAA had uncovered what it considered to be major rule infractions and that a substantial penalty was likely. The advice I had received from Cherry was that my answer to all questions from the media should indicate a lack of personal involvement in "knowingly or intentionally" committing any major rules violations. The assistant coaches had all resigned from their positions, and I think Cherry was still just trying to save my job. But I also understood that as the head coach of the program, I would be held responsible. Yet in terms of anything criminal, I felt certain no one on our current or former staff was culpable. On the basketball court, we had won our two exhibition games and were three days away from our regular season opener on November 27th when I got a call from the Baylor Vice President's office. Dr. Jim Netherton was requesting an immediate meeting with me and my attorney, on the morning of November 24th. We went to Netherton's office together where he and university counsel, Basil Thomson, were waiting. Netherton didn't say anything but handed me a letter. The letter was addressed to me and my counsel stating that my employment as head basketball coach at Baylor University had been terminated, effective immediately. The letter also referenced a small severance amount, as well as exit procedures. It was an ultra-short meeting and after leaving Netherton's office, my phone began blowing up with calls from the media. Word had gotten out before the meeting with Netherton had even concluded. Rather than answer phone calls and messages we scheduled a press conference for that afternoon.

The news conference was quickly put together with all the local media and a few out-of-town media sources in attendance, as well as some Baylor supporters, friends, players, and of course, Denna. I didn't need any coaching for the media ... with all the program scrutiny in recent months, I had become an expert in answering and deflecting tough questions. Asked about the timing of the decision I said it was "curious." The only breakdown I had was when asked what I would do now. I didn't have a real good answer for that because I was in uncharted waters. With my voice cracking, I said I didn't know, because it was the first time in my life since grade school that I didn't have a team. The media event lasted maybe an hour, after which Denna and I went home. I didn't know what I was supposed to do now. It was clear my time at Baylor and likely as a division one basketball coach, was over. But things would continue to get much worse.

The next morning, I received a call from local Baylor beat writer John Werner. I considered John a friend and he had always been fair in his reporting for the Waco Tribune Herald. I assumed John just had some follow-up questions about the events of the last few days.

The first thing John asked was if I had spoken with my attorney, David Cherry. I told John I had not seen or talked to Cherry since the press conference. The next words he spoke would change my life forever. "I'm sorry to have to tell you this, but you've been indicted by a federal grand jury." I couldn't believe what I was hearing and obviously had questions. John did not have much information to go on, but this is how I found out that I had been charged ... a phone call from a newspaper reporter. I ended the call with Werner quickly and called Cherry. He had just received word that I had in fact been indicted. Cherry quickly punted me saying he was not experienced or equipped to handle a criminal case, but that he would do some checking around on my behalf. It was a long day and all I could do was wait. I spent the day with Denna and my son Derek, trying to put it all out of my mind. I did not know what was waiting for me and had no clue about the upcoming process. I had been a college basketball coach with no experience in any criminal type of behavior and certainly was ill-prepared as a criminal defendant. I don't think I had ever even received as much as a parking ticket. I didn't want to see or talk to anyone. Late that night after business hours, I decided to go to the Ferrell Center arena and clean out my office. I figured I could get this done without anyone knowing or being around. I took boxes to my now former office and began packing up. About halfway through the process, there was a knock on my office door. It was Texas Football Magazine editor and writer, Dave Campbell with another reporter from the Associated Press. Dave and I had become friends, and he knew I wouldn't turn him down for an interview. But Dave wasn't really the interviewer, it ended up being the unknown reporter from AP that was asking the questions. It was a quick interview and mostly respectful under the circumstances. I remember him asking what was my most valuable possession that I was packing up and taking with me. I pulled out a playbook that I had been given by Mr. Henry Iba, former Oklahoma State and US Olympic team head basketball coach. Mr. Iba had been inducted into the Naismith National Basketball Hall of Fame in 1969 and was a legend in college basketball, having won national championships and Olympic gold medals with the U.S. team. Mr. Iba had passed away the previous year in 1993, and the playbook he gave me was in his own handwriting and was my most prized basketball possession in my office at Baylor. The reporter asked what I thought Mr. Iba would think about me now under these current circumstances. I didn't answer simply saying "I don't know." And the last question he asked was, "Are you prepared to go to a federal penitentiary for these alleged crimes." I sort of laughed and said 'no." That thought had never really even crossed my mind. The question came just a few hours after the news of the indictment had surfaced. I guess it was time to get real.

The next day I was in every newspaper and on every TV news show in the country. UPI released the following ...

WACO, Texas, Nov. 17 -- A federal grand jury Thursday indicted former Baylor basketball coach Darrel Johnson on fraud and conspiracy charges related to alleged attempts to gain eligibility for incoming junior college recruits. Also indicted were three former Baylor assistant basketball coaches and officials and coaches at community colleges in Texas, Kansas and Alabama. The legal action against Johnson came just one day after he was fired as head coach of Baylor's men's basketball team for alleged violations of NCAA and school rules during his two-year tenure. Johnson was charged with four counts of wire fraud, two counts of mail fraud and one count of conspiracy. The indictments allege that Johnson and others fraudulently attempted to gain academic eligibility for incoming junior college recruits for the 1993-94 basketball season. The U.S. Attorney's Office in Waco said the charges resulted from an investigation by the FBI, with the full cooperation of Baylor University, the Southwest Conference and the National Collegiate Athletic Association. Officials at Baylor University confirmed the indictments, but Mike Bishop, vice president for communications and marketing, said the school could not comment on the charges for legal reasons. Also indicted were former Baylor assistant basketball coaches Gary Thomas, Kevin Gray and Troy Drummond; Dan Pratt, head basketball coach at Kansas City (Kansas) Community College; Vinson Metcalf, head women's and assistant men's basketball coach at Hill College in Hillsboro, Texas; Humphrey Lee, dean of students at Shelton State Community College in Tuscaloosa, Ala.; and Jeanetta Hargrow, admissions and records officer at Shelton State. (UPI, 11-17-94)

    I had to leave Waco. The last thing I wanted was to be in the public eye. I was easily recognizable in Waco, and even throughout Texas and much of the country. Media attention on the case had been relentless, and images of me and my coaching career were plastered across television and newspaper outlets from coast to coast. I decided to go back home to Oklahoma City where my parents lived. They welcomed me back home but were probably more than a little embarrassed about what I was going through and the attention it was generating. Denna and Derek stayed in Waco with Denna finishing her master's degree. Derek was too young to know about anything that was going on with his dad. The first order of business was I had to get representation. I was facing the biggest fight of my life and needed an advocate. I reached out to Carol Hansen, the wife of my lifelong friend and mentor, Paul Hansen. Carol was an OCU law school graduate and had recently been appointed as an Oklahoma Supreme Court Justice. I wanted her opinion, her advice, and her help. She pointed me in the direction of Oklahoma criminal law expert and attorney, Garvin Isaacs. Garvin had a long history of practicing criminal law in Oklahoma and had worked on some extremely high-profile cases. Isaacs was also an OCU graduate and had been closely associated with the basketball program there. He had been close friends with former OCU coaches Paul Hansen and Abe Lemons. I contacted Garvin and we agreed to meet. Isaacs was sympathetic to my plight and seemed confident that we would prevail if the case went the distance. He agreed to represent me. Garvin would take the lead in the criminal case, with David Cherry providing some background and residual legal assistance, mostly from the NCAA and Baylor side of things. But I wanted to leave nothing to chance. A high school friend of mine, Jim Darnell, was practicing criminal law in El Paso. Jim had played high school football and went on to get his undergraduate degree at Dartmouth, and his law degree from SMU. Darnell and I been high school teammates in baseball, and played basketball together in junior high, winning an AAU national championship. Because of our long-standing friendship, I wanted Jim involved with the case. He agreed to join the legal team with the plan on him being in a subordinate, or second chair-type role. Hiring Darnell proved to be the best decision I ever made in my legal battles against the government. The team was on board, and we were ready to move forward with the case. Shortly thereafter, through counsel, I was ordered to surrender myself to the U.S. Marshall's office in Waco for formal booking and fingerprinting. This was serious stuff, and I was still somewhat in disbelief that I could actually be in this position. I was formally charged with seven felony counts of mail fraud, wire fraud, and conspiracy. I spent the next few months meeting with attorneys on a daily basis. Except for my interview with Michael Glazier, who was conducting an investigation on behalf of the Southwest conference, I was never interviewed or asked by government officials or the US attorney's office for testimony or an account of what had happened with regard to the charges levied against me. It's like they didn't even want to hear or consider another side of the charges. It became apparent that the U.S. attorney had no interest in trying to reach any kind of pretrial agreement. They wanted their day in court and would vigorously prosecute this case. My fate, my freedom and my future would be decided in a court of law with a twelve-person jury verdict.

"Many are the plans in a person's heart, but it is the Lord's purpose that prevails." Proverbs 10:21

CHAPTER 13 - THE TRIAL

It had been three short years since I was celebrating our second national championship amid a 54-game winning streak at Oklahoma City University. The jubilation of that moment had now turned into the fight of my life. The bewilderment of how all this could possibly happen was mind-blowing. In the course of a few months, my best player had been killed in an accident. I was fired from my dream job at Baylor, facing an NCAA and federal investigation, and now defending myself against seven felony counts in federal court with the real possibility of a long prison sentence. Attorneys representing me conducted their own interviews and investigations in preparation for our defense. Members of the Waco community had stepped up in a big way by establishing a legal defense fund to help pay for representation. It did not come close to covering all my expenses, but it was a big help and an indication of how Baylor supporters felt about me and this case. Despite all the attempts to criminalize the allegations made by the NCAA, the US Attorney's office, the Southwest Conference and the University itself, the local community was still supporting me. My efforts to assimilate into the Waco citizenry was paying dividends and hopefully would resonate with the prospective jury pool. The reason behind the NCAA investigating our program could be traced to a variety of potential sources. Maybe it was Bowers' making allegations against us or it certainly could have been based on the empirical evidence that the NCAA was retaliating against me for the Eric Manuel decision. But what was it that summoned the Fed's involvement and literally making this a potential criminal offense? There are several theories that make sense, but the motive given publicly was that it was just circumstance. Jim Fossum, an FBI agent living in Waco, said he had read about the allegations in the local newspaper, and for what is was worth, made a unilateral decision that the claims by the NCAA rose to the level of federal crimes. But the NCAA has long been littered with rule breakers that included coaches, university administrators, boosters, and student-athletes. Never before in the history of the NCAA had a major college head coach been held liable for rules infractions that would lead to criminal felony charges being filed. It was estimated that hundreds of NCAA member institutions had utilized the correspondence courses at Southeastern College of Assemblies of God for the eligibility of its student-athletes. This was confirmed by then assistant commissioner of the Southwest conference, Britton Banowsky, when he said in a public forum,

"This is definitely not just a Baylor thing. The academic abuses that may have occurred at Baylor likely occur at a great number of universities. They just haven't been discovered." (The Oklahoman, March 26, 1995).

This sudden gold mine of college credits apparently didn't raise a concern at SECAG, as they said they were happy there were so many new students from all over the country wanting to learn more about God.

"Dr. [Thomas] Wilson [the school's director of continuing education] said repeatedly that he was excited that junior college students were interested in studying the Bible," says Margaret Hennesy, director of alumni and college relations at Southeastern. "We thought of this as a way to reach people with the word of God." (Sports Illustrated, 11-28-94)

If you believe the account given by the FBI, this all occurred due to mere happenstance ... one of its agents reading about it in the morning newspaper. This would seem highly unlikely if not totally preposterous. But it is the story they gave. The Baylor coaches were the first in the history of intercollegiate athletics to be charged with federal crimes over recruitment and eligibility of players, and all because FBI Special Agent Jim Fossum read about it in the local paper.

Others facing indictment in the case were my three assistants, Troy Drummond, Kevin Gray, and Gary Thomas. Also indicted were the individuals who had served as test proctors for correspondence class exams. Humphrey Lee and Jeanette Hargrove were administrators at Shelton State Junior College in Alabama and were friends with Kevin Gray. Both had helped Gray in the past with the eligibility of student athletes when he worked as an assistant coach with the Crimson Tide. Also indicted were Dan Pratt, head basketball coach at Kansas City Community College, and Vinson Metcalf, assistant basketball coach at Hill College in Texas. I didn't know Lee, Hargrove, or Pratt, but Vinson Metcalf had played for me at Oklahoma Baptist University after transferring from the University of Idaho. I had helped Metcalf get the job at Hill and had helped him financially after graduating from college. Hill College was located just down the road from Waco, and Metcalf was frequently on our campus and had become friendly with our coaching staff. Each of the four defendants outside of our Baylor staff, had served as proctors for the correspondence exams of our four junior college recruits. The government attorneys had decided to try all eight of us at the same time, in one trial. It was likely the government's attempt to get each defendant lawyered up and looking out for their own self-interests while firing shots at the other defendants. And it worked to some extent. Each of us had our own individual counsel, all the while the US Attorney's office was making side deals to drop charges in exchange for testimony as a prosecution witness. Both Pratt and Metcalf went for it and had charges dismissed. They would both testify for the prosecution. Criminal attorneys will tell you that most people facing the possibility of prison will quickly change sides to the prosecution in exchange for amnesty. It was the four Baylor coaches and the two officials from Shelton State that would ultimately go to trial, each represented by individual counsel. I was confident with my team of Garvin Isaacs and Jim Darnell who would argue my case in court. Drummond's attorney was Asa Hutchinson who later became Governor of Arkansas and was a candidate for the 2024 Republican presidential nomination. All the defense attorneys seemed to be in agreement in their defense strategy. This included not letting any of the defendants testify, which is often the case in criminal trials, and placing the burden of proof on the government, which they felt would be highly difficult and improbable.

After four months of preparation with attorneys, co-defendants, and witnesses the case was going to trial. It would be heard by Walter Smith, an appointee by President Ronald Reagan as U.S. District Court judge for the western district of Texas in Waco. Smith had received his undergraduate degree from Baylor as well as his Juris Doctor in 1966 from Baylor Law School. The first step in the process was jury selection. The attorneys thought the trial would last over a month, but Judge Smith had different ideas. He was all about speeding up the process and after jury selection which lasted about a week, the actual trial was set to begin on March 27, 1995. My understanding of the interpretation of the law in this case revolved around the issue of what was called "specific intent." The defense attorneys seemed to feel this was a threshold the prosecution would need to clear … proving that it was in fact the defendant's "intent" to commit the federal charges of which they were accused. It was clear by now that NCAA violations had occurred within our program. But it was equally clear that no one was trying to break laws or defraud anyone. The prosecution attempted to make the trial about money, which is typical in these types of cases. The prosecutors from the U.S. attorney's office were John Phinizy from Waco and Dan Mills from Austin.

"In court, Mills said the coaches defrauded Baylor of scholarships and equated their actions to going into the BU administration building "with a gun and ski mask and making off with $50,000." (Dallas Morning News, 2-9-17)

The prosecution also put up witnesses from the University who corroborated their theory. Clyde Hart, Baylor track coach and compliance director, took the stand and said the motivation to get the players eligible for participation stemmed from greed. He spoke of the financial incentives for coaches of championship-level programs. His argument was that coaches helped players get eligible and defrauded the university out of a personal sense of financial motivation, to climb the coaching ladder and reap the fiscal rewards of upward mobility. James Netherton, Baylor Vice President, testified that the university stood to lose millions of dollars if the school went on probation because of rules infractions. It was clear that the prosecution was using money as the primary motivation for NCAA rule breakers. This strategy appeared to be consistent with the federal statutes on fraud. If a conviction was secured, mandatory prison time minimums would take effect based on the dollar amounts assigned to each specific count. If the prosecution could get the court to agree with the theory surrounding money, then each guilty count would likely mandate a potential five-year prison sentence, in addition to fines and restitution. What made matters even more dire was the fact that there was over a ninety percent conviction rate for multi-count federal indictments. It would be possible that the prison sentences could be served concurrently, but it was looking like a guilty conviction would produce a minimum of five years in the penitentiary.

The two key witnesses for the US attorney were Dan Pratt and Vinson Metcalf. Both were basketball coaches, Pratt at Kansas City Community College and Metcalf at Hill College in Texas. Both had served as exam proctors for our recruits and had been part of the original indictment that was handed down including them as defendants charged with multiple counts. Both coaches had agreed to testify for the prosecution in exchange for immunity. Metcalf had played for me at OBU and had come to me beforehand saying he wanted to talk about the case. He was visibly scared at the idea of his prosecution and was not at all himself when we met. It became apparent later that he had already made the immunity deal and likely requested a meeting with me at the behest of the prosecution trying to get me to say something incriminating that could be used in court. When I informed my attorneys that I had spoken with him, they were concerned and said he was most likely wearing a wire. Metcalf went on to testify at trial that I had told him to *"be strong, stick to his story, and tell the truth."* Although I didn't remember the exact specifics of what I said, his testimony was substantially accurate. The prosecutor tried to focus on the "stick to your story" aspect of the story while insinuating that it was telling him to lie. The defense obviously wanted to accentuate the "tell the truth" discourse which of course was self-explanatory. Metcalf finished his testimony on the witness stand quoting John 8:32, "The truth shall set you free." Upon cross-examination one of the defense attorneys called him on it with the question, "Don't you mean testifying for the prosecution shall set you free?" It was one of the more poignant points of the entire trial. Vinson had been a former player and a friend, whom I had greatly helped in his career pursuit. And here he was testifying in court against me. I don't particularly think that Metcalf's testimony hurt my case or any of the other defendants, and I understand his reasoning for making the decision. But it was disappointing. Coach Dan Pratt's testimony wasn't too damaging either. He had very little evidence of any wrongdoing. He testified on the stand that no one had asked him to help the players pass the exam, and no one had told him to provide answers to the test. He simply said that when Gary

Thomas had asked him to proctor an exam, Coach Thomas had said how important it was to obtain a certain passing grade. He said he knew what that meant. In the end, Pratt and Metcalf escaped government prosecution and provided minimal damaging testimony for the prosecution.

One could make the case that Judge Walter Smith should have recused himself from the case, being that he was a Baylor graduate. None of us knew what side of the case he would come down on, but most who knew him felt he would follow the law, regardless of personal affections or feelings. All we wanted was a fair trial, and for all of this to end. I was confident then as I am now, that there was no violation of federal laws in our program. On April 1, 1995, the prosecution called their final witness and rested their case. I had no idea about the protocol of a jury trial and had never even stepped into a courtroom before. But after the prosecution rested, all six of the remaining defendants filed motions to dismiss all charges, stating primarily that the prosecution had failed to make its case. Judge Smith made some important decisions before the defense presented their case. It was apparent that Smith didn't like this case and was looking for a legal precedent to dismiss. He said more than once to defense attorneys, *"Bring me a case,"* citing the need for precedent. The attorneys all tried to find some sort of legal precedent, but as Jim Darnell said to the court, "There simply are no cases." This case was groundbreaking and uniquely unprecedented. Smith did however dismiss all counts against Lee and Hargrove, administrators from Shelton State that had served as exam proctors. He told them that the decision to dismiss was obvious and that the government had not even tried to make a case against the two defendants. He admonished the prosecuting attorneys in open court, while granting the motion to dismiss, "with apologies from this court." This left just the four Baylor coaches remaining as defendants. Without legal precedent, the proceedings against the four of us would continue. But Smith also made another important ruling, basically removing the "money theory" from the record. He did not agree with the testimony of the Baylor officials that money was a key issue. There was no financial consideration as a basis for any coach's conduct, even if it was in violation of NCAA rules. This was huge because it likely gave the court some discretion in sentencing if there were convictions. The mandatory minimums in prison time would not necessarily apply without the financial factor that the government and Baylor officials had tried so hard to imply.

As the trial continued, defense attorneys for the four defendants were in basic agreement to not allow their clients to testify. They also felt strongly that the prosecution had failed to make its case of fraud, and there was no need to put defense witnesses on the stand. It appeared that Judge Smith was tipping his hand a little by dismissing all charges against Lee and Hargrove, as well as the ruling that removed the financial motivation of the defendants as a primary cause. The defense was confident enough to proceed straight to closing arguments. But I was having a side battle with my lead attorney, Garvin Isaacs. I was dissatisfied with Garvin's performance as far as cross-examination of the government's witnesses. He was obviously an accomplished criminal attorney, but I just didn't think he was resonating with the jury. Many of his questions on cross resulted in successful objections from the other side. I had a meeting with Jim Darnell about it and asked him to finish the case for me and to deliver closing arguments. Jim agreed to do it but warned me that it could send a bad sign to the jury changing attorneys in midstream, indicating some sort of internal dissension. But I was adamant ... I wanted Darnell to finish for me.

The next day I asked Garvin if we could go for a car ride to get some alone time and talk about the case. He agreed. We went to dinner in a quiet place outside of Waco where we could talk. It was there that I told him of my decision, that I wanted Darnell to close. Isaacs warned me of the consequences of making this change in the middle of the trial, just as Darnell had. He thought he had established a rapport with the jury, and that our best chance of winning was for him to make the closing remarks. But my mind was made up, Darnell would finish. The more we talked; the angrier Garvin became. He had spent a significant amount of time during the trial appearing on talk shows, and making TV appearances on my behalf, while Darnell and I would pour over the different facets of our defense. Both were likely needed, but I felt Darnell better represented my interests, maybe because we had been friends for almost thirty years. Isaacs became agitated and wanted to leave the restaurant. He was driving the car back to Waco and it was mostly silent when he pulled off to the side on Interstate 35 as we entered back into town. He stopped the car and told me to get out. He didn't want me in the car with him. The last thing he said to me before he drove off was that he would meet me in the judge's chambers first thing in the morning. I walked back on the side roads of I-35 to where we were staying. Six months prior I had been the head basketball coach at Baylor University and the toast of the town. Here I was now, walking alone on the interstate trying to figure out how everything had ended up so badly. We were on the downside of the trial and now it felt like my own attorney had turned against me, with my freedom and livelihood very much in question. It was one of the lowest points of my life.

The next morning Darnell and I went to meet Isaacs in the judge's chambers. Garvin explained to Judge Smith what was happening. Smith said that as the client, it was entirely my decision but cautioned me about making this decision in mid-trial. But the decision was made. Isaacs was still upset but promised to stay in court until the conclusion of the trial, so as not to adversely influence the jury. Smith told him he agreed with that decision and that it was an honorable and commendable thing to do. But I will never forget the last thing Isaacs said to Judge Smith. He looked him in the eye and said that I had promised him he would be in charge of the defense and that it was obvious that Mr. Johnson was not an honest man. I couldn't believe what I was hearing. The attorney who was supposedly representing my best interests, told the man that would sentence me if convicted, that I was dishonest. Darnell was also in disbelief. Isaacs didn't speak to me for the rest of the trial but did remain in the courtroom until after closing arguments. It was now up to Jim Darnell to finish strong.

The attorneys for my three assistant coaches all agreed not to put any witnesses on the stand. But Darnell wanted to put up a single defense witness on my behalf. Chip Land, owner of the Oklahoma City Cavalry would testify and confirm the offer he made me to coach the Cavs. He would give specific details about the compensation agreement that was offered to me, which hopefully would put an end to the idea that anyone was motivated by financial considerations. Chip testified that his offer could in fact surpass my compensation package at Baylor. He also testified that I had told him I turned down the offer because "I had done nothing wrong at Baylor and needed to defend myself against these accusations." The prosecution quickly objected to this part of the testimony on the basis of hearsay. The objection was sustained and stricken from the record. But Chip did a great job, and I think maybe affirmed the judge's decision that money was not at the central part of the equation. The point of his testimony was that if it was about money, I had a golden parachute as a way out and declined it. After Chip's testimony, all four defense attorneys rested their case, and the trial proceeded to closing arguments. It had been a grueling and stressful year of preparation for the trial, and now it was coming to a close.

"For I know the plans I have for you, plans to prosper you and not to harm you, plans to give you hope and a future." Jeremiah 29:11

CHAPTER 14 - THE VERDICT

Each of the defense attorneys gave a heartfelt and compelling closing argument to the jury. The main point from each was that yes, NCAA rules violations had been committed, but that nothing rose to the level of a federal crime. I found it ironic that the court could not dismiss the cases because there was no legal precedent, but the prosecution was free to bring a case before a jury that had no precedent. Perhaps it was just a layperson's logic, but it seemed odd. The defense attorneys hammered home the lack of specific intent. They argued that there could be no crime without some kind of intentionality. The defense was doing its job, addressing the allegations of criminal intent based on the law. It was not their job to argue NCAA violations or even the ethics of cheating in major college sports. They were trying to create enough reasonable doubt with the jury to get verdicts of not guilty and keep their clients out of prison. Jim Darnell did a magnificent job in closing to validate my decision to put him in charge. This case was personal to Jim. We had been friends for a long time, had played sports together, attended the same high school, and had similar backgrounds. Plus, I think Jim really believed in me, even if I had taken a wrong path with the NCAA stuff. His closing was passionate and near the end, he broke down. With his voice cracking, he finished the closing with the confirmation that he had known Darrel Johnson for thirty years ... and that he knew Darrel Johnson was innocent. The jury had to be moved by his comments and by his emotions. I was too scared to be emotional, and the whole thing was kind of a blur to me at this point.

The prosecution was passionate as well in their closing. They stated their interpretation of the law which was obviously quite different from the defense. One of the things that stood out in U.S. Attorney Dan Mills' closing remarks was his reference to patriotism, insinuating that it was the patriotic duty of the jurors to bring back guilty verdicts. He asked what the jury truly felt about their government. If it was their thoughts that the government would bring an unworthy case before them, then they should "let 'em go." It was a persuasive argument that would likely resonate in small-town America, where the citizenry was mostly conservative, patriotic, and pro-law enforcement. Now, the testimony and argument phase of the trial was over. Judge Walter Smith gave instructions to the jury based on the ways to interpret the various laws and statutes, and what issues were most critical in arriving at a verdict. The court recessed and the jury left for deliberations.

Rumors were flying as the trial was winding down. We had heard speculation that there was someone on the jury who was dug in for acquittal on all counts. The defense only needed one juror committed to a not-guilty verdict. But without any direct knowledge, it was impossible to know what these twelve individuals were thinking. Each day of the trial that we left the courthouse we were met by a throng of reporters from all over the country. It was the lead sports story in the news almost every day of the trial. We were staying at a secret, undisclosed location to avoid the news media, and there were days when we would leave court through the back door hoping to go unnoticed. After closing arguments, Isaacs had left, presumably going back to his home in Oklahoma City. It was just me, Denna, and Darnell together during the time period of waiting for the verdict. Coincidentally it was at the same time as the NCAA Final Four in Seattle. My brother Phil was coaching at Arizona at the time and was in Seattle along with almost every other major college basketball coach in the country. We spoke almost daily during the trial and on Final Four weekend I told him that the case was wrapping up and we expected a verdict soon. He caught the first flight he could get out of Seattle which was not an easy task with the finals going on. I found out later that he had to pull some major strings to get on a flight. Darnell and I had watched the finals on TV as UCLA won its eleventh straight national championship. I broke down in tears for the first time while watching the game. Maybe it had finally dawned on me the enormity of what I had lost, being a part of the game that I loved so much. Phil arrived the next day on Tuesday. It felt good to have someone else with me that was on my side. He would stay with me through verdict day. On Wednesday, April 5, 1995, we received word that the jury had reached a verdict. We were to reassemble back at the courthouse that afternoon.

Darnell had a lot of experience in criminal trials and had learned how to read juries. If there was eye contact from jurors with the defendant, it was a good sign. It was like I had seen on television a million times. The jury returned to the room, and I saw no eye contact. The bailiff asks everyone to rise as the judge enters the courtroom. He asks the jury foreman if they had reached a verdict. He said they had. He began by reading the case number as my heart pounded. All of the defendants were standing. I am reminded of a biblical passage in the book of Luke when Jesus actually sweats drops of blood in the garden of Gethsemane. Scientists and doctors affirm that it is entirely plausible for Jesus to be so agitated, so traumatized, and in so much pain that he might actually sweat blood. I didn't do that but every cell in my body felt like it was going to explode as the jury began to read the verdict. It had all come down to this moment. My life, my freedom, and my future were in the hands of these twelve men and women. It was a long way from coaching two national championship teams and putting winning basketball programs together. This was the day that would change my life forever. I prayed. The jury foreman began the reading of the verdict …

In the case of the United States of America versus Darrel Johnson we find the defendant:

In Count 1 – Not Guilty
In Count 2 – Not Guilty
In Count 3 – Not Guilty
In Count 4 – Not Guilty
In Count 5 – Not Guilty
In Count 6 – Not Guilty
In Count 7 – Not Guilty

Darnell grabbed me and his first words were "There is a God!" I was too numb to be excited or to have any emotion at all. It was over and I was found not guilty on all counts. The victory was sweet but shallow because all my assistants had been convicted on various counts. Drummond and Thomas were composed, but Kevin Gray sobbed. I found my brother and we fell into each other's arms, both openly sobbing inside the courtroom. I went to try and console my fellow coaches, but they wanted nothing to do with me. Their lives had been changed forever as well but in a much different way. I think all of the defense attorneys were surprised by the guilty verdicts. In my opinion, the assistant coaches were wrongly convicted and should win on appeal. But going through a criminal investigation and subsequent trial is an education. The most important and startling thing I learned was that no one involved in the case seemed to care much about the truth. The attorneys on both sides just wanted to win, the judge wanted to rule in such a way as to not be overturned on appeal, and the witnesses were mostly just looking out for their own self-interests. I watched witnesses lie that took an oath to tell the truth and I watched attorneys spin the truth and the facts to help sway the jury. Overall, it still appears to me as an example of a colossal failure of our judicial system. I was absolutely not guilty of the crimes of which I was accused, and neither were my assistant coaches. If they were guilty, then so was I. I had been the head coach of a program that had gone awry, and to some extent lost its way. But the kids and the staff were good people. Looking back, the responsibility was mine and no one else's. The judge quickly set a date for sentencing and adjourned. Jim Darnell suggested we leave the courthouse through the back entrance, but I wanted no part of that. I grabbed Denna by the hand, and we walked out of that courthouse through the front door to a throng of TV cameras and reporters. My brother Phil and my attorney Jim Darnell walked with us. We didn't answer any questions and made no comments. This long and traumatic ordeal was over in a sense. I had spent the better part of the last year of my life preparing for trial, with lawyers, and in court. But during this time, I needed to be focused, and I had a mission to prove my innocence. Every day was filled with preparation, meetings, discovery, witness statements, pouring over documents and strategizing. What would I do now? I had no direction, no plans for after the trial, and no job or income. I was a basketball coach without a team and without any financial means.

Prior to the trial and with the help of Mike Glazier, Baylor had self-imposed sanctions and penalties in the men's basketball program, hoping to mitigate the punishment that was sure to be levied by the NCAA. Included in the sanctions were loss of scholarships, forfeiture of revenue, and a ban on post-season play for a period of several years. President Reynolds released the following press statement through the media relations office at Baylor,

"We hope this action will be seen for what it is-a public statement and condemnation of the serious misconduct involved in

this case, and an unmistakable message that actions of this kind will not be tolerated at Baylor University."

The NCAA has a long history of putting schools on probation that had broken its rules. But very often the punishment does not fit the crime, and those punished played no part in the actual NCAA transgressions that had taken place. As a case in point, the junior college players who were the subject of the investigation all transferred to other schools and continued their basketball careers. The players who remained at Baylor could not compete in postseason play for years because of the apparent misdeeds of others. They were the real victims in the case. Some of the players at Baylor had not even been in the program at the time but would pay the price levied by the NCAA. They were punished severely and had done nothing wrong. The Baylor attorneys and administration threw the coaches under the bus and assigned blame to no one else. With guilty verdicts at trial, it was hard to argue the innocence of the coaching staff, and everyone at Baylor did their best to distance themselves from the four of us who had been indicted. People in the community that I considered die-hard and lifelong friends disappeared from my life. It's incredible the lengths some will go to in the interest of self-protection, and to run away from the "guilt by association" premise. With the convictions of my three assistants, Judge Smith scheduled sentencing for July 7th … they would have to wait four months before finding out their fate in sentencing. As expected, all three men filed appeals of the verdict, which ultimately were upheld in superior court. Drummond, Thomas, and Gray also disappeared from my life. With the verdicts that were handed down, it seemed we were now on different sides. They were in self-protection mode as they faced the real possibility of significant prison time. But no one could blame them for adopting an "every man for himself" posture with all that had transpired. While I admittedly enjoyed a certain sense of extreme relief with the not-guilty verdict for myself, I felt a strong sense of responsibility for what had happened to them. It was me that had brought them to Baylor, with hopes and dreams of competing for championships and advancing their coaching careers. And now it had all come crumbling to the ground. As I saw it, we were all guilty of rules violations, but none of us were guilty of federal crimes. Yet I was the only one that had not been convicted. Hoping to mitigate the penalties for the assistants, I released a statement to the press before sentencing, that as head coach at Baylor, I accepted all responsibility for improprieties that occurred in our program. The statement was true, I should be held accountable as the head coach. There were others at the university that escaped penalty and public scrutiny, but the buck had to stop somewhere. Taking sole and ultimate responsibility for the violations in our program was the right thing to do, but it would most likely signal the death of my coaching career.

Sentencing day came on July 7, 1995. While I wanted to be there for my assistants, Darnell advised me not to go. As hard as this entire ordeal had been for me, I could only imagine what the other three men were feeling on this day. The emotional, physical, and financial toll had drained all of us. But now they were in court to face their uncertain future, with their freedom on the line. Darnell felt like the Court never liked this case and was somewhat baffled that the government ever brought it to trial. US Attorney John Phinizy had asked the Court for a sentence of five years in a federal penitentiary and a $250,000 fine for each convicted defendant. In the end, Judge Smith was sympathetic and departed from the mandatory minimum prison sentences that could have been imposed. Most fraud cases involve money or other financial assets. Smith cited the law that allowed the departure since there was no monetary exchange or fraudulent activity that involved money. Gray, Thomas, and Drummond received a $1000 fine, community service, and a year of probation. And while I'm certain they were relieved about no prison time; they would carry the stigma of convicted felons for the rest of their lives. The court case was over for all of us. It was time for us to move on with whatever was next. I had Denna and Derek that were of paramount importance, but I also wanted to resume my coaching career. I would do so much differently this time. Maybe I would have a chance with the not guilty verdict and a record of accomplishment with my teams. But the first step would be to try and clear my name with the NCAA infractions committee. This would be a near-impossible task with the NCAA's record of success against those who questioned their authority or fought against their decisions. There was also the Eric Manuel case that loomed large with the NCAA. The deck was stacked against me, but this game had been my life, and my love for the game only grew stronger after being forced out. My case with the NCAA Committee on Infractions was set for August 11, 1995, in Monterey, California. The trial was over, but I was still fighting.

Making history -1972 Undefeated State Champs

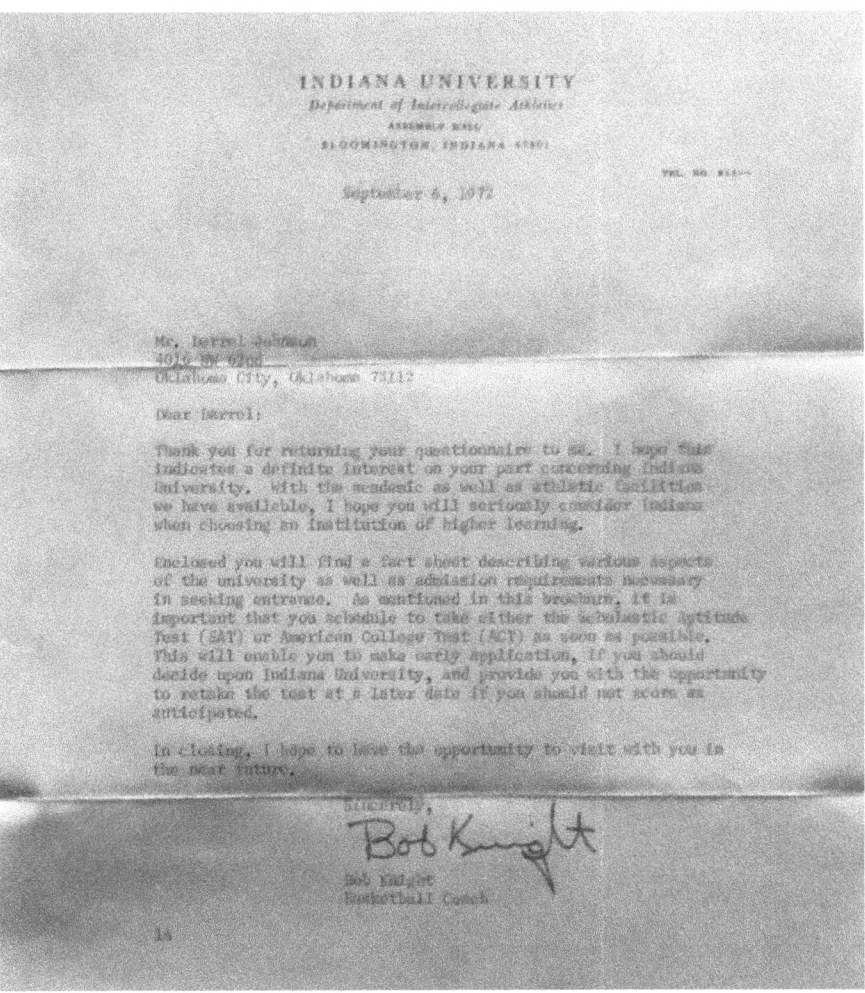

Coach Bobby Knight calling.

Battling on the collegiate hardwood with former teammate Alvan Adams

The worst moment of my college career

OBU Standout Charged With Delivering Cocaine

Murray Evans
June 21, 1989, 12:00 a.m. CT

SHAWNEE Calvin Moore, the leading scorer and rebounder for the Oklahoma Baptist basketball team last season, is free on bail after being arrested Friday night and charged with the unlawful delivery of crack cocaine.

Moore, 22, has claimed that he is a victim of mistaken identification by Shawnee police. He has been suspended from the basketball team and the university, where he was attending summer school, pending the outcome of an OBU investigation.

"Calvin has been suspended until this matter is resolved to our satisfaction," OBU athletic director Norris Russell said. "We are conducting our own investigation into the matter in an attempt to support what the Shawnee police are doing.

Wrongfully accused

Oct. 5, 1990

Manuel Supported By Sutton

By Jerry McConnell
Staff Writer

Oklahoma State coach Eddie Sutton testified Thursday it would be a great injustice if Eric Manuel were barred from playing college basketball.

The testimony came in a trial before Oklahoma County district court judge William Henderson on Manuel's suit seeking to prevent the NAIA from barring him from playing basketball for Oklahoma City University. The trial will resume today.

Sutton was Manuel's coach at Kentucky when the NCAA held that Manuel had cheated on a college entrance exam and ruled he was ineligible to compete at Kentucky or any other NCAA school.

"Eric is a marvelous young man and a great athlete," said Sutton. "To this day I still don't believe he did anything wrong. It's very likely something did happen on the test, but in my opinion he knew nothing about it."

Manuel dropped out of Kentucky after two years and enrolled and played basketball last season at Hiwassee College, a two-year school in Madisonville, Tenn., from which he graduated. Recruited by several

See MANUEL, Page 25

Manuel

From Page 21
NAIA schools, he was later signed by OCU.

"The NCAA is the governing body for about 900 colleges and universities, including the so-called majors. The NAIA is the governing body for about 500 other schools, most of them small state and private institutions.

The NAIA has ruled that Manuel is ineligible to compete at any NAIA school on the basis of a rule that says any student who has completed eligibility at a four-year school is ineligible for further college participation. The NAIA thus held he had completed his eligibility at Kentucky because he was no longer eligible to play there.

"I was shocked that the NAIA would not accept him," said Sutton. "I feel there has to be compassion for him."

Manuel's attorney, Mark Hammons, contended that the NAIA spells out its definition of completing eligibility, which included either graduation or four years of participation or enrollment for 10 semesters, but did not mention being ruled ineligible by the NCAA.

"We've got rapists, convicted criminals and convicted drug dealers playing in the NAIA," said OCU coach Darrell Johnson. "It's completely unfair to bar Eric."

Sutton and Johnson testified that Manuel has a chance to become an NBA player, but likely couldn't make it unless he were allowed to continue his college career. The 6-6½ Manuel was regarded by some sources as one of the top five recruits in the country when he graduated from Southwest High School in Macon, Ga., in 1987.

Manuel's suit also named OCU as a defendant, but OCU officials said they were in sympathy with the suit and wanted Manuel to be able to play for the school.

Late in the day, NAIA attorneys asked for a directed verdict when it developed that an OCU scholarship officer had apparently not signed the scholarship agreement until that afternoon.

OCU officials said they no longer required the officer to sign the agreement, although an "old" form specified the officer must do so. Chris Mauldin, an OCU vice president, testified that OCU considered it a valid agreement.

The judge decided that the case would resume at 9 a.m. today, when the NAIA will put on its witnesses.

— AP Laserphoto
Eric Manuel listens to testimony Thursday in an Oklahoma County court.

Coach Eddie Sutton testifies

Back to back National Champions

Iconic photo of Eric Manuel hanging in the OCU arena

The moment of jubilation after winning it all

THE WHITE HOUSE
WASHINGTON

March 25, 1991

Through the thoughtfulness of Senator Don Nickles, I have learned that the fans of the Oklahoma City University men's basketball team are honoring the squad for winning the 1991 National Association of Intercollegiate Athletics National Championship. It gives me great pleasure to join you in recognizing the Chiefs for this noteworthy accomplishment.

This championship reflects the outstanding efforts of all those involved in the OCU basketball program. From the dedication and hard work of the coaching staff and the players to the steadfast support of the fans, this winning season is an achievement in which each of you can take justifiable pride.

Barbara joins me in sending our congratulations and best wishes. God bless you.

George Bush

Letter from President George Bush.

HE ALWAYS HAD FIRE IN HIS BELLY

Baylor's new basketball coach was raised on competition. His teammates remember him as a tough, smart player, and his college teams have a similar reputation

By JOHN WERNER
Tribune-Herald staff writer

Growing up in Oklahoma City in the 1960s, Darrel Johnson was a baseball fanatic. His favorite player was Oklahoma native Mickey Mantle, the Commerce Comet.

If Johnson had his way, he would have played baseball all the way through college and perhaps into the majors. Wouldn't it have been great to hit a home run in Yankee Stadium, just like his boyhood hero?

"Baseball was my first love," said Baylor's new head basketball coach. "I stayed with it as long as I could and we even won a state championship my junior year at Putnam City High School. I played pitcher and outfield. But really, I wasn't good at either of them."

Some dreams end. But others begin.

Long and winding road

At the age of 37, Johnson is one of the youngest major college coaches in the country. Baylor hired him last month to try to turn around a program that has had three losing seasons in the last four years.

He's come a long way from coaching and driving the bus at Hefner Junior High in Oklahoma City 14 years ago. Before arriving at Baylor, he made stops at two high schools and three colleges.

"I probably did it the hard way," Johnson said. "I started at rock-bottom by coaching a junior high team. I've swept gym floors and have driven kids home on the bus. I moved up through the ranks. I think the experience has made me a better coach and a better person."

Playing was serious business

When Johnson was 10 years old, he got his first taste of success when his YMCA baseball team won the Oklahoma state championship. Even then, Johnson's father, J.T., noticed his son approached sports more intensely than most kids.

"Most kids at that age like to goof off a lot," said J.T., who coached the YMCA championship team. "But Darrel and the group he was with was different. They were very intense. They were very aggressive and competitive and wanted to do well."

Baseball was definitely Johnson's sport. He played in summer leagues, and was usually one of the best players on his teams. But basketball was another matter. When he went

Please see JOHNSON, Page 4D

Staff photo — Bobby Sanchez
Darrel Johnson begins Baylor career on a roll after winning 54 straight at Oklahoma City.

A dream and a five year contract.

Darrel Johnson

What could have been.

Darrel and Denna Johnson leave the Federal Courthouse in Waco after the verdict.

Darrel with mentors and coaching legends, Paul Hansen and Abe Lemons.

Darrel with NBA legend Jerry West at the Clippers training facility.

4B   Houston Chronicle   Friday, Nov. 19, 1993

Baseball/College basketball

Baylor eligibility flap leads to boycott

By JONATHAN FEIGEN
Houston Chronicle

The Southwest Conference and Baylor officials declared four Baylor basketball players ineligible Thursday, prompting coach Darrel Johnson to boycott Thursday night's game in protest.

In a statement issued by the SWC, the league announced that the players, all junior-college transfers, would be ineligible to play "pending a complete analysis of their eligibility status."

The statement said the league and school are "engaged in a joint inquiry into matters related to the men's basketball program which involve possible violations of NCAA legislation."

SWC commissioner Steve Hatchell met with Baylor president Herbert Reynolds in Waco on Monday.

The possible violations involving the four suspended players are unrelated to allegations of rules violations brought by Baylor women's coach Pam Bowers.

Jason Ervin, a guard from State Fair (Mo.) Community College; Tyrone Davis, a center-forward from State Fair; Marcus Thompson, a guard from Westark (Ark.) Community College and Shannon Brantley, a forward from McLennan Community College were not in uniform for Thursday's exhibition game against Arkansas Express, which the Bears won 103-95.

Ervin and Davis were expected to start for Baylor at point guard and center, respectively. Thompson was competing with Willie Sublett for the starting job at small forward.

"The conference is taking an active role in this matter," Hatchell said. "In this case, it is important as a precautionary measure to ensure all eligibility issues which have been raised are fully resolved prior to the student-athletes competing."

Johnson issued a statement Thursday arguing the players should not have been held out of Thursday's game.

"I'm not in attendance at tonight's game in support of the four players whose eligibility has been delayed," Johnson said in his statement. "It is my belief that these student-athletes are eligible according to all Baylor, Southwest Conference and NCAA rules.

"However, we welcome any inquiry into the conduct and activity of our program and look forward to a quick resolution to this matter."

Assistant coach Kevin Gray served as head coach Thursday.

Johnson did not return calls Thursday.

Hatchell would not comment on the league's investigation, but said a detailed release would be issued when the school's and league's investigations are complete.

The Boycott – standing strong.

BU stunned by Banks' death

Sophomore's tragic loss staggering blow to already shaken program

By JOHN WERNER
Tribune-Herald staff writer

The tragic death of forward Jerode Banks leaves a deep scar on a Baylor basketball team already deeply scarred.

During the past year, the Bears have been under investigation for everything from academic fraud to illegal inducements. They've watched players leave the program almost on a weekly basis throughout the summer.

And now, the worst possible news. One of their brightest young stars died in a car accident.

Banks' death was confirmed by Department of Public Safety officials Friday after they received positive identification of the body from the Southwestern Institute of Forensic Sciences in Dallas.

The 20-year-old sophomore from Temple was killed after his car crashed into a bridge support and burned near Bruceville-Eddy early Thursday morning.

The funeral service will be held Monday at 1 p.m. at First Baptist Church in Temple. Branford-Dawson Funeral Home in Temple is handling the arrangements.

"Everything that we've been through pales in comparison to a tragedy like this," said Baylor coach Darrel Johnson Friday evening. "This is devastating."

Johnson said that Baylor players called him throughout the day on Friday. Most of them were in shock. No one wanted to believe that a teammate and a friend had died.

"Most of them just had a numbness," Johnson said. "In a situation like this, you go through all kinds of emotions. They all feel pain, sorrow and grief."

"All I feel now is frustration," said Baylor guard Aundre Branch. "We've all had to go through this investigation and now this happens. I just don't know what to do."

People who saw Banks on the last night of his life said that he was happy and enjoying himself. Banks stopped by the Temple High School gym to play

Please see BANKS, Section Back

Tragedy strikes BU basketball.

> **Counter Copy**
>
> FILED NOV 17 1994
> CLERK, U.S. DIST. COURT
>
> IN THE UNITED STATES DISTRICT COURT
> FOR THE WESTERN DISTRICT OF TEXAS
> WACO DIVISION
>
> UNITED STATES OF AMERICA, • CRIMINAL NO. **W94CR117**
>
>   Plaintiff, • I N D I C T M E N T
>
> V. • [Vio: 18 U.S.C. 371 --
> Conspiracy to Commit Mail and
> DARREL JOHNSON, (1) • Wire Fraud; 18 U.S.C. 1341 --
> GARY THOMAS, (2) • Mail Fraud; 18 U.S.C. 1343 --
> TROY DRUMMOND, (3) • Wire Fraud; 18 U.S.C. 2 --
> KEVIN GRAY, (4) • Aiding and Abetting]
> VINSON METCALF, (5) •
> JEANETTA HARGROW, (6) •
> HUMPHREY LEE, (7) •
> DAN PRATT, (8) •
>
>   Defendants. •
>
> THE GRAND JURY CHARGES:
>
> INTRODUCTION
>
> At all times material to this Indictment and to all Counts in the Indictment:
>
> 1. The National Collegiate Athletic Association determined eligibility standards for all participants in Division I-A athletic basketball programs.
>
> 2. As these eligibility standards pertained to two year college transfer athletes, certain requirements were established for eligibility to participate in intercollegiate basketball for a National Collegiate Athletic Association Division I-A Institution.
>
> 3. The National Collegiate Athletic Association and the Southwest Conference imposed limits on the number of basketball scholarships that could be awarded each year by Baylor University.
>
> 4. The number of basketball scholarships that Baylor University could award for the 1993-1994 school year was thirteen.
>
> 5. The value of each basketball scholarship at Baylor University for the 1993-1994 school year was in excess of $10,000.00.
>
> 1

Grand Jury Indictment.

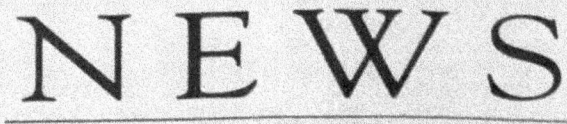

FOR IMMEDIATE RELEASE
(Nov. 16, 1994)

BAYLOR TERMINATES MEN'S BASKETBALL COACH

WACO, Texas -- Baylor University today terminated its employment of men's head basketball coach Darrel Johnson, effective immediately, and launched a search for an interim head coach to guide the team through the 1994-95 season.

Assistant coach Harry Miller will conduct team practices and will coach the Bears in the season opening exhibition game Friday, Nov. 18, in Waco against the Brazilian National team, according to Dr. James S. Netherton, Baylor Vice President and Chief Operating Officer for Administration and Planning.

Netherton said he terminated Johnson's contract following a determination that "the program or those associated with the program had violated the policies and procedures of Baylor University and the rules, regulations, or policies of the NCAA." When informed of the decision, Baylor President Herbert H. Reynolds stated that he concurs with Dr. Netherton's decision.

Netherton declined to go into any details of specific allegations surrounding the Baylor men's basketball program, saying that the University will submit a comprehensive self-report of program violations to the NCAA in the next few days. This report is consequent to the self-imposed sanctions on the men's basketball program announced recently. The NCAA will determine what details of Baylor's report will be released.

-30-

JOHNSON/TR-1, CT, METRO/MB

The end of a career.

SPORTS

Former Baylor Coach, Assistants Indicted on Mail Fraud Charges

L.A. Times Archives

Nov. 18, 1994 12 AM PT

FROM ASSOCIATED PRESS

WACO, Tex. — A federal grand jury Thursday indicted fired Baylor basketball coach Darrel Johnson, three former assistants and four others on mail and wire fraud charges.

The indictments came one day after Johnson was fired by school administrators who determined the men's basketball program had broken school and NCAA rules.

The charges accuse Johnson and assistants Gary Thomas, Kevin Gray and Troy Drummond of conspiring with junior college officials to commit postal and wire fraud to gain eligibility for incoming recruits for the 1993-94 season.

Baylor Coaches Facing Federal Prison.

NEWS

Darrel Johnson Denies Wrongdoing; Trial Begins Monday

Stephen Power
March 26, 1995, 12:00 a.m. CT

WACO, Texas - Faked tests. Phony term papers. A possibly improper recruiting scheme. To some, the case against Baylor University's former basketball coach sounds like fodder for the NCAA. In Waco, it goes by another name: United States v. Darrel Johnson.

Johnson, the 39-year-old former Baylor coach, goes on trial Monday with five co-defendants in U.S. District Court on charges of participating in a mail and wire fraud scheme involving recruitment of five junior college basketball players. Legal experts said they know of only one other case in which a college coach has been charged with a federal offense stemming from alleged NCAA rules violations.

Johnson, the former coach at Oklahoma Baptist and Oklahoma City University who lives in Houston, could not be reached for comment.

Getting ready for trial.

Declared eligible by the NCAA ... the Baylor 4 never played a minute for Baylor University.

Former Baylor Coach Acquitted; Assistants Guilty

Thu., April 6, 1995

X   ✉ Email   ⊙ Reddit

Compiled From Wire Services

Former Baylor University basketball coach Darrel Johnson was acquitted, but three assistants were convicted in connection with their recruitment of five junior college players in 1993.

A federal jury found that, although Johnson was responsible for the basketball program, he was unaware of improper help his assistants gave to enable the recruits to pass classes they needed to enroll at Baylor.

Johnson, indicted one day after Baylor fired him in November, was acquitted of all seven counts: four counts of wire fraud, two counts of mail fraud and one count of conspiracy.

His assistants, Gary Thomas, Troy Drummond and Kevin Gray, were found guilty of various charges of wire and mail fraud.

They face up to five years in prison and fines of up to $250,000 on each of the wire fraud and mail fraud counts.

Prosecutors had accused the Baylor coaches of helping the five junior college players make higher grades by providing them term papers written by others and changing grades.

The mail fraud and wire fraud charges were filed because the U.S. mail and fax equipment were used in the process.

The jury began deliberating the case late Monday following almost 5 hours of summations from attorneys in the case.

A bittersweet verdict.

Coaching my son, Derek (State Champs 2008 and 2009).

"The Lord is close to the brokenhearted and saves those who are crushed in spirit." Psalms 34:18

CHAPTER 15 - BROKEN

It was hard to imagine a life without basketball. I remember all the way back to Taft Junior High School in Oklahoma City skipping lunch to shoot hoops during lunchtime. I would think that this could be my life. I loved it so much, even then. I had been a star high school player, an average college player, and then a low-level professional player in Europe. My coaching career had produced championships at every level, and I had my shot as a Division One head coach. Truthfully, most coaches never get that kind of opportunity. I had been blessed in a career that far surpassed my abilities. Some of the best basketball coaches I've ever known are not necessarily those at the highest level of the sport. As I approached my meeting with the NCAA, I knew the odds were against me ever coaching again at the major college level. I just wanted back in the game that I loved so dearly. It didn't much matter the level or the job itself. I was happy when I was coaching in high school and in small college, so maybe that was a possibility. First, I needed to try and clear my name with the NCAA.

The 1990's version of the NCAA is far different than it is today. There was no real due process afforded to coaches who challenged NCAA sanctions. The NCAA enforcement staff is the equivalent of the prosecutor in the modern-day American justice system, and the infractions committee equates to judge and jury. The two arms of the organization are not only friendly with each other, but they fraternize, socialize, travel and vacation together. There was no real system of checks and balances in the NCAA process, and accountability for their decisions and rulings was mostly nonexistent. Add to that the fact that some of those on both sides of the process had been involved in the Eric Manuel case, and one could surmise that I had no real chance. I had been given a five-year show-cause requirement by the organization, which prevented me from coaching at an NCAA member institution during that time frame. The enforcement staff and infractions committee would get together several times each year to adjudicate various cases that had been brought to them. They always met in expensive resort-type locations, and it was mostly a party atmosphere for the NCAA executives and they were all on a first-name basis. They would play golf, go to parties together, participate in beach or mountain outings, and mix in a smaller amount of time for meetings. My appearance before the NCAA infractions committee would be held in Carmel, California in one of the fanciest resorts I had ever seen. After the costs of the trial, lawyer's fees, depositions and other expenses I was flat broke. I could not afford the trip to Carmel but my attorney and friend, Jim Darnell told me to "just get there." He was reducing or waiving his fees by this time because he knew I was out of money and had no income. So, I found a way to get to Carmel. I didn't know that the committee was not only hearing my case but also that of Baylor University. The school had self-imposed sanctions and penalties but needed to make their case before the committee that they had gone far enough, and that no further punishment was warranted. But the NCAA would have to approve the steps they had taken. So, the meeting in Carmel was extremely divisive and confrontational. They had made a large hotel ballroom into a courtroom-like setting. The enforcement staff sat together on one side of the room with the infractions committee on the other. In the middle of the room, there were large conference tables set up for Baylor administrators, staff, and their team of attorneys. Adjacent to the Baylor contingent there was a small table for Darnell and me. It was a contentious setting that reminded me of congressional hearings. What I was most surprised to see was two of my former assistants, Gary Thomas and Kevin Gray, sitting with the Baylor contingent. Both would make witness statements on behalf of the university, and it appeared to me that Thomas and Gray had been recruited by Baylor to help them with their case before the committee. Their testimony was damaging to my appeal before the NCAA, but I could hardly blame them for siding with Baylor, especially if it had helped them with sentencing before Judge Smith. I never spoke during the proceedings and Darnell was my one and only advocate. He did a spectacular job in front of the committee, even if it was against overwhelming odds. I remember this day as one of the most difficult days of my life … in a room fighting for my livelihood and feeling like everyone else in the room was an adversary. I left Carmel thinking my career in basketball was likely over, in spite of Darnell putting up a good fight against the NCAA. I was found not guilty in the courtroom, but Baylor attacked me from every angle trying to mitigate NCAA sanctions against the university. They spent most of the day affixing blame towards me, and self-aggrandizing their compliance efforts and self-imposed penalties. They used the fact that they had self-imposed probation to try and persuade the committee to lift the post-season ban by one year. As it turned out, this was a smart strategy employed by Baylor. Impose harsh penalties against yourself and then throw yourself at the mercy of the NCAA and ask them to reduce the sanctions you had self-imposed. The meeting with the NCAA ended with decisions on the requests and appeals to be determined.

Denna and I had sold our home in Waco, and she had accepted a geologist job in Houston. We had enough equity in the Waco house to make a down payment on a house in The Woodlands, a suburb on the north side of Houston. Denna became the breadwinner, and I spent most of my time trying to find a job in basketball. Needless to say, my life had become a train wreck and Denna and I were struggling in our marriage as well. I had no job, had spent all our savings on attorneys and defending myself, and had a seriously low level of self-esteem and sense of self-worth. Depression had set in with no real sense of direction or purpose. Denna was still supportive and we might have made the relationship work if I had just devoted this time to my family. But I was caught up in trying to get back into basketball and had become a lousy husband and father. Denna eventually filed for divorce, and I moved back to Oklahoma City.

Moving seemed like the logical thing to do at the time. I needed to find a job, a place to live, and a direction for my life. My parents lived in Oklahoma City, and I had friends there from high school. I began dating an Oklahoma girl which resulted in a brief marriage. With all the turmoil in my life, I had no business getting married or even dating really. This rebound marriage was the product of having no real direction after losing most everything that included my job, career, financial wherewithal, and reputation. I was depressed and rudderless and had no chance of any success in an interpersonal relationship. But one great thing came out of this short-lived marriage and her name was Lauren Paige Johnson. The birth of my daughter in 1999 was a complete blessing from God and certainly helped in my pursuit of living a purposeful life. But her mom and I split up soon after her birth, and I was given joint custody. I was clueless about how to take care of a baby girl, but I learned quickly. My weekends were now alternating between going to Houston for visitation with Derek and staying in Oklahoma City to spend time with Lauren. After completing real estate school, I obtained a license and began to dabble in the business. Between my trips to Houston and time with Lauren, I would carve out time to try and learn the real estate game. It was tough going and the learning curve and transition from coaching to real estate was significant. My relationship with Lauren's mom had become contentious and I had to fight to see my daughter. But Denna knew how much Derek needed his dad in his life, despite our differences. She never held a grudge against me and made co-parenting easy, even with the distance between us. In between trips to Houston, we would talk on the phone and Denna was great about keeping me informed and including me in his activities. If you had to be divorced, it seemed like we were doing the best we could being active in our son's life. Real estate was paying some bills, and I coached a traveling all-star team back when college teams were playing exhibition games. It was only for a few weeks, but I still had that love of the game. The NCAA made its ruling in my case in September 1995, only a month or so after the meeting in Carmel. The strategy used by Baylor had worked ... the committee had reduced the post-season ban by a year. The ruling cleared me from most of the violations that had occurred, but the thing that kept the show cause restriction in place was what they called a "lack of institutional control." The NCAA said I had failed to adequately monitor the program. This was a fair ruling in my eyes, but Darnell was determined to take this all the way to a conclusion and wanted to appeal. I agreed to go forward, and we filed an appeal with The NCAA Infractions Appeals Committee. This is the first time I had ever heard of this committee, but it was the final step in the process with the NCAA.

Baylor was happy with the NCAA's ruling and particularly with the reduction of the post-season ban. But I don't think they were happy with how the committee ruled on my appeal. They likely knew that the "lack of institutional control" finding could resonate back to other departments at the university as well. Baylor had settled a multi-million-dollar suit with women's coach Pam Bowers and the last thing they wanted was another lawsuit from me. The Baylor lawyers decided to take preemptive action.

Less than two months after the ruling by the NCAA Committee

on Infractions I answered a knock on my door at home in Oklahoma City. It was a stranger looking for Darrel Johnson. After identifying myself he handed me a folder and said, "You've been served." I was being sued by Baylor University for just under a million dollars. The lawsuit document said that I was responsible for Baylor losing millions of dollars due to my failure to adequately monitor the basketball program during my tenure at the school. I sat down in disbelief … and cried.

The story hit the wire almost immediately. It was extremely calculated and released through Baylor Media Relations,

WACO, Texas - Baylor University believes it is appropriate and necessary to protect its rights under the terms and conditions of its written contract with former head men's basketball coach Darrel Johnson. Therefore, Baylor University has filed suit against Johnson in the United States District Court for the Western District of Texas. In that suit, Baylor seeks to hold Johnson responsible for losses sustained by Baylor as a result of Johnson's conduct in the men's basketball program.

After pulling myself together I called Darnell. He was surprised but felt like this was a ploy on the part of Baylor which amounted to emotional blackmail. They had to know that I had no money, and they had zero chance of collecting anything. But he said that with the NCAA's recent ruling along with our pending appeal, Baylor was likely afraid of another lawsuit for wrongful termination and one that could potentially implicate others at the university. He calmed my fears for the moment, but it was just another public embarrassment and a dark moment on this continued road of despair. I let Darnell handle any negotiations with Baylor, and we rarely talked about it. We were both more concerned about the upcoming appeal with the NCAA and a final attempt to have the "show cause" restriction lifted. According to Darnell, after speaking with Baylor University counsel it became clear that Baylor was not really at all interested in pursuing the lawsuit. Pretty quickly, Baylor attorneys made an offer through Darnell. They were prepared to drop the suit if I would agree not to sue them. Darnell was against it saying that I had a legitimate cause of action against Baylor, and his advice was to not give away that option. It was sound advice, but after all that had happened, I just wanted it to end. It was still my hope to win the appeal and someday in the future be free to coach college basketball again. I thought if I sued a former employer, it would seal my fate as far as coaching in college again. So, I agreed, and Baylor dropped the suit. The Baylor press release said afterward…

"Baylor University believes the purpose of its suit has been fulfilled and feels that no additional purpose would be served by continuing to pursue its claims."

Nothing had changed at all except that I had agreed not to sue the university or any employees. And that was the University's only real purpose in filing the suit.

We began preparing for our meeting with the NCAA Infractions Appeals Committee, which was scheduled for early 1996, in Jackson Hole, Wyoming. The appeals committee was smaller and met in a more intimate setting. This was just Darnell and I along with the committee, and Baylor attorneys who were mostly just spectating. The only thing left to appeal was the "lack of institutional control" and the show cause sanction. The appeals committee seemed to be a more legitimate entity to me. Darnell was his usual brilliant self in making our case. As we wrapped up the meeting the committee asked me if I wished to address the members. This was a bit of a surprise since I had not been given the opportunity to speak at the meeting in Carmel. I had nothing prepared, but I said yes and stood up to my feet. The committee was comprised of university officials from other schools, law scholars, faculty representatives, and administrators. I looked at each one of the committee members before speaking. And with a cracked voice, I told them … "This process has gone on for more than two years. I've lost my job, my career, my reputation, and my family. I've spent all of my resources and earnings in defending myself. I've answered every question asked of me and I've been put on trial in a court of law. I've been subjected to public humiliation, embarrassment, and intense public scrutiny. Make no mistake, I've messed up and I've broken some rules. Some of the allegations levied against me have been true, but I can honestly tell you that many have not. And no matter what you believe to be true here today I can tell you this … I've been punished enough."

This was about as raw as I've ever been. It was unplanned and spontaneous … but I believe these committee members could feel my pain and heartache as my voice trembled and tears poured down my face. The meeting was adjourned, and Darnell and I were leaving when I felt a hand on my shoulder from behind. It was Roy Kramer, chairman of the Southeastern Conference and renowned godfather of college football. "Coach I appreciate your words. And I promise we'll be fair." I thanked him and we left. Later that day Darnell and I parted ways, and I went back to Oklahoma City. All we could do now was wait for the decision. And pray.

If anything good can come out of something like this I have found that for me, I began leaning on God. My prayer life, church attendance, and bible study were at an all-time high. I went back to my roots at Quail Springs Baptist Church, where Pastor Charlie Graves was still preaching. He had performed my baptism in the church more than twenty years earlier. I had professed my faith in Jesus at the age of 15, but now I became closer to God than ever before. Charlie was anointed by God and a mentor for me as my faith grew. I had lost so much, but there was so much more life to live. I turned to God. And it was in September of 1996 that we received the final ruling from the NCAA Appeals Committee.

"Trust in God with all your heart and lean not on your own understanding." Proverbs 3:5

CHAPTER 16 - TRUST THE NUDGE

It had been more than two years since I last coached at Baylor University. The investigation, trial, and NCAA appeals had lasted more than three years. Finally, in September of 1996, we would get the final ruling from the Committee on Infractions Appeals. Coaching again was unlikely, irrespective of the NCAA ruling. Too much time had passed ... and the negative publicity had been widespread, damaging, and overwhelming. So, the decision from the appeals committee had lost a high level of importance and significance. I was hoping for the best, but realistically, it would probably have no effect on my future in basketball. I had given everything I had to the game and to the profession, and it was over. My priorities had shifted toward my family in Houston, my little girl, and my walk with God. But there was something else that was stirring inside me. I felt a Godly presence like never before, to the point of a personal relationship, which I believe God wants with all of us. Still trying to find my way in the real estate business, I felt God wanted more from me. I could feel a push, a nudge, a sort of whisper from the Holy Spirit. I felt a pull to be closer to my son, Derek. But how could that be? We had a good relationship, and, in some ways, I was a much better dad to him now than I was when I was married to his mom and living in the same household. Divorce is a crushing blow to so many families, but sometimes the separation actually creates more committed parents. Denna was a great mom, but she was working full time, had her own set of friends, was active in church and had a social life ... but it all took a back seat to being Derek's mom. She also saw the transformation in my own life with more commitment and emphasis on being a good father, and a renewed Christian faith. Could God be calling me to go back to Houston? No way, I thought. I had started a business in Oklahoma City, and I had parents, friends, and a baby daughter there. I didn't know anyone in Houston except Derek and Denna and saw zero job prospects there. Plus, I had no money. So, I fought with God about it. I said no. It made no sense. I was still seeing Derek every other weekend and on holidays, which would be exactly the same even if I lived closer. God continued to stir my soul, and I continued to find good reasons to say no. But the more I grew in my faith the more certain I became that it was in fact, God speaking to me. He continued to convict me, push, and nudge to the point that it would not go away. The more I said no, the stronger the nudge. I was still searching for a new career and a new direction in life when I got the call from Jim Darnell. In the midst of God's spirit moving me, the final decision on our appeal had been delivered. The committee's ruling hit most national media outlets on September 21, 1996. From wire reports and associated press via the Oklahoman:

"Darrel Johnson got some good news from the NCAA last week. The Oklahoma native had his penalty stemming from the basketball problems at Baylor University reduced from five to three years.

Johnson, 41, will be able to return to coaching at an NCAA institution on April 15 of next year. Johnson coached Oklahoma City University to two straight NAIA championships and was head coach at Oklahoma Baptist University prior to guiding Baylor to 16-11 finishes in 1992-93 and 1993-94. Allegations of players receiving fraudulent grades for correspondence work surfaced during Johnson's tenure at Baylor and led to his dismissal. Johnson was found not guilty on seven counts of conspiracy and mail and wire fraud in federal court in Waco, Texas, in 1994. Three of his former assistants were convicted and received three years of probation. In the latest action, the NCAA Committee on Infractions determined there was not sufficient evidence to conclude that Johnson was guilty of academic fraud or unethical conduct."

We had won, though it's hard to claim victory with all that had been lost. But Jim Darnell had won. He had been relentless in seeing this through, well after I would have given up. The NCAA said I could coach again, but I still doubted it would ever really happen. Most importantly, the fight was finally over. The struggle had taken its toll on my life as I had known it. There was enormous loss, depression, stress and anxiety, some of which would have lifelong consequences. The financial and emotional cost was staggering, and it took away this game from me that was once the love of my life. I was elated with the news, and I still had that love for the game. There was a small sense of personal redemption, but no one really noticed. The story of my legal battles and appeals with Baylor and the NCAA seemed to have captured the attention of the national media for the better part of three years. The story was highlighted everywhere and frequented front-page news in major media outlets. What was almost amusing was the fact that the story of my successful appeal was buried somewhere near the obituary pages in the local newspaper. It was not nearly as newsworthy or appealing as the trial, the accusations, the lawsuits, and the uniqueness of a major college basketball coach who had lost everything. But life had taken some different turns now, as well as some new meaning. My walk in faith was strong and it still felt like God wanted more from me. It seemed like He was leading me down a new path apart from coaching. The internal fight continued about the mere idea of moving back to Houston to be closer to Derek. I could come up with a multitude of reasons why it was a bad idea, but the most compelling one to go could be found in scripture: "Blessed are the ones who hear and obey God's message." Luke 11:28

There was no doubt in my mind that God's message to me was clear … go be with your son. There were plenty of times in my life when I had been in obvious disobedience to God's word and paid no attention to his message. It was likely that I had never been close enough to God to hear His voice or have the ability to understand His ways. My way had always been the first option and then ask for God's blessing or ask Him to save me from whatever impending crisis I had created for myself. But this time was different. My way hadn't worked out all that great. And as much as I resisted, the message stayed constant. If I was going to be a fully devoted follower of Jesus, I would have to act in obedience to His will and His path for me. It was time to put up or shut up and just trust. I needed to stop fighting and arguing with God and surrender in obedience. I didn't have a plan, and I didn't know God's plan … I just knew He wanted me to go. So, I let go and began making plans for the move back to Houston to be with Derek in his most formative years.

I had spoken with Denna about the idea and that I was feeling led to come back. She was all in favor of it. She obviously had her hands full being a single mom with a flourishing career in full throttle. She welcomed the help with Derek but more importantly, she knew the value of Derek having his dad more active in his life. But how was I going to manage this? I prayed fervently, seeking divine guidance for every step of the way. I had never trusted God in such a blindly obedient manner. There had been moments of obedience in my life, but mostly only when God's plan appeared to align with mine. I had no job waiting for me in Houston and I had no money for rent or to buy a home. Yet somehow, I believed. I believed in God's plan and the clarity of his guidance. This would be a gigantic leap of faith, but I felt the assurance from God's word that I was on the right path.

I had some retirement that had built up and I thought I could live on that for that for a while. So, against the advice of my CPA, I cashed out of all my retirement funds to buy a home in Conroe, about fifteen minutes away from where Derek and Denna were living. Maybe I could find a coaching job, teach private lessons, or continue some real estate business. The most important thing was to be a part of Derek's life. I could go to teacher conferences, watch him play sports, participate in his activities and hopefully be a role model. I had been absent for much of his life, both physically and emotionally, by chasing a career that was self-centered and all-consuming. It was way past time to make up for all of that. There were a few loose ends with the real estate business in Oklahoma that my mom graciously took off my hands. It was so hard to leave Lauren, but I pledged to do everything I could to stay active in her life. My parents fully supported the decision to be back in Houston with their grandson. It took a while to put it all together, but when the house was ready for me, I loaded up the U-Haul and headed south from Oklahoma City. I had no idea what lay ahead.

"And we know for those who love God all things work together for good, for those who are called according to his purpose." Romans 8:28

CHAPTER 17 - WHERE IS GOD?

Derek and Denna helped me move into my new home in Conroe. The grace, selflessness, and forgiveness of my ex-wife are unsurpassed in this world. With all that had been lost, the loss of my family was what hurt the most. The blame lies squarely on me, as my priorities had been misplaced during my marriage to Denna. I could never make up for that, but with God's help, I could try. With a new home in a new city, I set out to make a new life. I made friends with neighbors, joined West Conroe Baptist Church, and tried to be socially active. But most of my time was spent looking for work, participating in Derek's life, and neighborhood and church activities.

Even with a not-guilty verdict behind me, a successful NCAA appeal, and a pedigree of championship-level basketball, I still could not get a sniff at a coaching job. The damage was done, the publicity had been stifling, and my reputation was tarnished. As much as I wanted to move on from basketball, it was in my blood, and it was still hard to let go. I taught a few private lessons in the local area and worked a lot with Derek. He was tall, as both his parents were, and was 6'3 in the eighth grade. He showed lots of potential and seemed to love the game as well. It was great being around him and participating in his development, as a young man and as an athlete. I had made some great friends through a singles group at the church but there was a lingering problem … I was running out of money and needed employment badly. I applied for everything in basketball that was even marginally local and actually garnered some interest from a small country high school that was located just outside of The Woodlands and was looking for a basketball coach. I applied, did my best to recruit the administration, and was given an interview. It was exciting to think about the possibility of coaching again, even at a small-town high school. I went into the interview knowing that I was vastly overqualified for the job and would likely have only one issue.

The Baylor fiasco and subsequent criminal trial would follow me wherever I went. These were the tough questions that I would need to address to potential employers, no matter what the level. But I absolutely nailed the interview and left thinking I was going to get the job. They made no promises except to follow up with me in a few days. The next week I was invited back for a second interview. There would be some teaching responsibilities as well as the coaching aspect, but I had kept my teaching credential active and held a master's degree in education. With that going my way as well as the success on the court of the teams I had coached, I felt confident. They certainly would not have any candidate with more experience or anyone who had demonstrated a higher level of success in terms of wins and losses. My record as a coach was stellar. But I had a big black eye with the misdeeds in our program at Baylor. I was a one-issue candidate. But I felt a camaraderie with the administration and in my estimation, had another great interview. I was experienced with the hiring process and thought I knew what to say, and when to say it. The school superintendent said they would call me with their decision on Friday. With all the interviews I had been through, I felt an ability to read the room and could predict the likelihood if I was their guy or not. My confidence in getting the job was extremely high. I was their guy.

This was not a dream job by any means, but God had brought me here to be with my son. That would be my primary focus no matter what job I had. At this point, I found myself enthused about the idea of coaching again in a small town, close to Derek, and watching him grow. I became more excited about what God was doing with my obedience, faith, and trust. This was perfect … I was beginning to see God's plan now. He was giving me another chance at coaching this game I loved, and at the same time being an integral part of my son's life. I began planning. I researched the team, the schedule, the league they played in, and the talent level. I started planning a preseason development program and some ways to provide continuity between the high school and the lower grades. I planned ways to be active in the local community and to be a spiritual leader at the school and with my players. The juices were flowing again! I hadn't even been formally offered the position, but I was getting my swagger back. Things would be different this time around. It wouldn't just be about winning. We would concentrate on the intangibles of things like character building, living with integrity, teamwork, sacrifice, and spiritual growth. God would be in control this time, and we would seek to honor Him with everything we did. It was a perfect plan.

The anticipation of waiting until Friday for the phone call from the school was daunting. I wanted to tell everyone of the plans I had for the total program. This was going to be far more than just coaching a basketball team. We would be a model for other programs to follow, making contributions on and off the basketball court. I had worked myself into quite a lather over the endless possibilities of this program. It was Friday afternoon that I got the phone call. It was the athletic director of the school. He sounded somber. He informed me that the school had decided to go in a different direction with their coach. He thanked me and wished me luck.

At first, I was just surprised, and then it became devastating. I lost it. This was my last shot. I didn't understand. It just couldn't be. I was doing everything right and was committed to God's will. I walked out into my front yard in the middle of this Friday afternoon deflated and hurt. I dropped to my knees, sobbing and shaking my fist at God. Maybe for the first time in my life, I had truly been obedient to my creator. God had brought me here. I knew that in my heart and soul. Why? Did he really have a plan at all? Was this just an extension of the downward spiral I'd been on for three years? I started yelling towards the heavens ... "I'm here because of you ... I was obedient. My heart is where it should be. I've lost everything, there's nothing left. Where are you, God?"

I was mad at God, I guess. But this was the end of hope for me. I had no other plan, no agenda, no safety net, nothing. I had no money, no income, and no job prospects. I felt I had lost everything, and this was my last chance. It was a total meltdown that had been created by the rejection from the school, and I was feeling sorry for myself. After shaking my fist at God and screaming at the heavens, I finally calmed down after a while. That night I was recomposed and went to God in prayer. I asked for forgiveness for my earlier antics of the day and said that I was wrong, I hadn't lost everything. I had God and I had that little boy that just needed his dad. I was fiercely disappointed to be rejected by the game again after all these years, but deep inside I knew still that I had done the right thing by following the Holy Spirit in obedience. And it was at that moment that I think I finally realized I couldn't do this on my own. My love for the game didn't matter anymore and my hopes, dreams, and future plans were unimportant. I had to abandon myself and surrender everything to my Lord and Savior. My plans were noble and God-honoring… but they were my plans, not His. I went to sleep that night in peace, having finally given it all away. It was a complete surrender and submission. I had no idea where we were heading from here, but I felt God's presence again. I prayed in earnest, Heavenly Father … your will be done. I give it all to you. Abraham Lincoln once said in a time of crisis, "I have been driven to my knees many times by the overwhelming conviction that I have nowhere else to go." At this point in my life, I turned to God … because I simply had nowhere else to go.

The night was restful as if a burden had been lifted. It wasn't mine anymore. Basketball was obviously not in my future, but I was making peace with that. I had given my all to the game and it had been costly, and it was time now to give my all to Jesus. I woke up Saturday refreshed and ready to start a new life. I surrendered my love of basketball to God, along with everything else. The bills still needed to be paid but God had never failed to provide. I thought about mowing yards and starting a business. I thought about teaching or giving lessons. I still was not sure where we were going but I believed that God still had a plan. I was reminded of God's promise in Hebrews … "I will never leave you nor forsake you." Either I was a believer, or I wasn't. God would not abandon me.

It was Saturday morning less than 24 hours after getting the rejection phone call from the school and the subsequent meltdown in my front yard when I received a phone call. It was a voice I didn't recognize that introduced himself as Kenny Williamson, director of player personnel for the Charlotte Bobcats, the NBA's newest expansion team. I had met Kenny briefly a few months earlier at a basketball event in Dallas when he was a scout for the New York Knicks. There were rumors that he was getting a promotion by going to the Bobcats. He quickly got to the point of his call, to offer me a college scouting job with the Charlotte Bobcats. I couldn't believe it! Less than 24 hours after being turned down by a small high school in Texas, I was getting an offer from an NBA team. I was in total shock and before I could get a word out of my mouth, he said there were two conditions that would need to be met before I could accept. First, he said I needed to understand that they were going to work my tail off. The team had two draft picks but there was no team until the next season. We would spend the entire year scouting college and international players in preparation for next year's draft. I would concentrate mostly on college players and would travel coast to coast watching and evaluating draft prospects. I would personally attend a minimum of three games per week during the season, not counting tournaments, TV games, and film study. I'd also be responsible for conducting background checks on each prospect that was on our draft board. The second condition was a big one he said and was non-negotiable. They needed me to live and work out of Houston! I was speechless. Are you kidding me? The day after I finally gave up on basketball and the day after I surrendered everything to Jesus, I got the job offer of a lifetime. This is the NBA, the highest level of basketball in the entire world. The offer came out of nowhere ... and they want me to live in Houston. Actually, there can be no doubt, argument, or discussion about where this came from. This was all part of God's plan. It was His gift to me, but first, my heart had to be changed. This was an absolute miracle from God.

I enthusiastically accepted the position with Charlotte. Kenny Williamson would be my immediate supervisor, and the general manager was former NBA player and legend, Bernie Bickerstaff. The team was owned by Bob Johnson, founder of BET Television, with a guy named Michael Jordan as one of the investors of the team. A day earlier I had been ready to start a new career at a small high school outside of Houston, and today I had become an NBA scout. I could not wait to get started. I was back in the game, and I was telling everyone. The downward spiral of the past three years into the deepest, darkest depths of despair seemed to be over. After all the pain, heartache, sadness, depression, and loss ... I now had a dream job in the NBA, was active in Derek's life and development, and had a personal relationship with Jesus that never before could have been comprehended. But this was way beyond just getting my dream job. This was about transformation. I was a new man ... a new creature in Christ with a changed heart. God was giving me an amazing second chance at life, and to forge ahead on His path.

I went to work for the Bobcats with unbridled excitement and a little bit of nervousness that we all face in a new job. Every experienced college coach thinks it would be an easy transformation to become an NBA scout. We know the game inside and out, we know how to recognize talent, and we know how important the intangibles are in building a championship-caliber team. But I quickly learned how much I didn't know about making the leap from college to professional basketball. You analyze the game from a completely different perspective. It's especially challenging when you're watching a high-level college game with multiple prospects on both teams. It was my job to give an evaluation of the player's offensive and defensive abilities, his ability to impact the game, and other skill set attributes like ball handling, rebounding, passing, effective athleticism, and decision-making. Then there were the intangibles to assess. Things like attitude, team-first mindset, work ethic, coachability, body language, and basketball IQ. But it was also part of the job to project what level of pro he could become. We had tiers of projection categorized as a franchise-type player, a core player, a starter on a championship team, a rotation-type player, a roster filler, or a developmental type of player that could be stashed in the developmental league or overseas. We also would need to assess our specific team needs and determine if the player was a good fit for our team, our coaching staff and our style of play. We would compile mock draft rankings and do our best to determine what players might be available at our pick. This would entail a large amount of intel, calling on friends, colleagues, and sources around the country to obtain information. There was a lot more to the job than I had envisioned, but I loved every minute of it. What made it even better was the group I was working with. The Bobcats had put together a stellar front office, coaching staff, scouting staff, and player personnel department. Kenny Williamson was right; they did in fact work my tail off. I spent the next year of my life on the road for the Bobcats and at home spending time with Derek. The gloom and doom of the past three years was now just a bad memory. My new life was absolutely perfect. God is so incredibly good! But more changes were on the horizon.

"And to put on the new self, created after the likeness of God in true righteousness and holiness." Ephesians 4:24

CHAPTER 18 - CHANGING THE CULTURE

Before taking the job with the Bobcats, I had been teaching a high school health class at The Woodlands Christian Academy (TWCA). It was just across the street from Derek and Denna and got me out of the house for a few hours each week. It paid almost nothing, but it helped me become a part of the community. I kept teaching the class while traveling with my new NBA job but had to get it covered by a substitute teacher on the days I'd be gone for work. It was a great school with high academic standards and a pricey tuition. I particularly liked it because I could see Derek after school every day that I was home since he just lived across the street, and I strongly believed in the value of a faith-based Christian education. The kids at the school were great and I became friends with some of the other teachers and administrators. But my main focus was Derek, my job with Charlotte, and continuing to walk in faith. My first year working in the NBA was exhausting, eye-opening, and thrilling to say the least. I loved the job and the people I worked with. We drafted Emeka Okafor out of Connecticut with the #2 pick and began building around him with expansion players that were made available as well as free agents. Our team wasn't very competitive at the outset but that was to be expected. Derek was beginning to show real promise as a basketball player and I loved watching his development while working with him. He was in junior high school in The Woodlands and playing summer basketball on a traveling squad. I ended up coaching his AAU team in the summer since that was a slow time for my NBA job. This was just another example of how my obedience in following God's plan by moving to Houston was paying dividends, as this never would have happened otherwise. God's perfect plan had taken shape, and I was overjoyed with every aspect of my new life and starting over. During one of our summer basketball trips, I received a call from the head of school, John Echols, where I was teaching the health class. He asked if I could come meet with him at the school when I returned to Texas from our trip. I agreed but had no idea what he wanted. I thought maybe he was going to take the health class away from me since I was having to be gone so frequently. With all my travel during the school year, this would be understandable. But we set up an appointment and I went to see Echols at the school when I got home. The purpose of the visit was totally unexpected.

Echols told me their basketball coach was leaving the school and asked if I would be interested in taking over. Wow! I had not thought much about coaching again since I took the position with the Bobcats. The offer was more than flattering but my answer to Echols was "No." I loved what I was doing in the NBA and didn't want to give that up. He understood and we said goodbye. But the next day Echols called again and invited me to come back in and talk about this further. My mind was made up, but I had great respect for Echols and for the school, TWCA, and agreed to meet again. Echols said he had talked with the board and would like me to reconsider. But this time he made it a lot more tempting. He knew how important my NBA job was to me and said I would be able to hire two assistant coaches, and I could keep my job with the Bobcats. Basically, I would be at practice and at games when I was not on the road, and when I was traveling my assistant would serve as head coach. It was an interesting concept, and I asked Echols for a couple of days to consider it. TWCA was a mid-level private school in terms of enrollment and sports participation and had only existed for about ten years. Their football program was doing well but basketball had been dismal and had never experienced a winning season. Echols and the board were striving for excellence in all their academic and extra-curricular pursuits and saw an advantage of having an NBA scout and someone with my experience on board. I didn't see a real downside to taking the job, as long as it didn't adversely affect my travel schedule for scouting. But I had a hidden agenda as well.

TWCA was losing in basketball for an obvious reason ... their talent level of athletes was low. In Texas private schools, you can take students from any location and in any school district. Schools don't like to use the word "recruiting," but it definitely happens. At TWCA, there were no scholarships or financial aid for student-athletes. They had to pay the same tuition as all other students. But having taught a class at the school for a year now, I saw the potential impact a Christian school could have on kids. They attended chapel every week and were required to take classes in Old and New

Testament as well as apologetics. It was a different atmosphere from the public schools for sure. Academic expectations at TWCA were high, with a better-than-average record of college acceptance. In the back of my mind, I thought this would be a great option for Derek, but he had established himself in his current school, and it would be a hard sell to both he and his mom. In the meantime, I accepted the coaching job at TWCA.

Admittedly, one of the reasons I accepted the job was hoping to bring Derek with me. He was a rising star on the basketball court and if he came, it might entice other talented players to come as well. But it was way more than that. There was no one on the planet more qualified to coach my son than I was, and there was also no one else who cared about him as much as I did. The idea of seeing him every day and being a part of his basketball journey would be another dream come true. And I genuinely believed it would absolutely be in his best interest. It took some persuading, but Derek and Denna were on board. Derek would begin school at TWCA as a ninth grader.

Derek was by far our best player, even as a freshman, but there were a couple of other guys who could play a little as well. There was also some interest from players on the summer travel team that I coached as I had thought might happen. But for the most part, TWCA was an expensive school option, and there was a "wait and see" attitude among those who were even marginally interested. But I loved this little school and especially loved seeing my son every day in a Christian setting. God's blessings continued and I was convinced that I was walking in His path that he had laid out for me. As assistants, I brought Joel Bishop who had been Derek's junior high coach in public school, and Bill Storey, a retired coach that I had met through summer basketball. Storey was a basketball lifer much the same as I was and had a deep love of the game. We hit it off immediately and found ourselves on the same page in virtually everything we did. This was so vitally important since Storey would be in charge when I was on the road. So, we had to fine-tune our coaching methods so that the players would have confidence in both of us. Travel to college games started again in October of Derek's freshman year at TWCA. It was hard being away, but I absolutely had the best of both worlds. I had two full-time jobs and loved them both. I would literally land at the airport in Houston and go straight to the school, then head back to the airport for my next trip a day or two later. It was busy and exhausting, but so incredibly fulfilling and blessed. TWCA posted its first winning season in the history of the school in 2005, won the district championship and made it to the 3A state tournament, before losing in the quarter-finals. The Bobcats had traded its first-round pick to get Okafor the previous year, who was now on his way to NBA stardom. Without a first-round pick, we drafted Bernard Robinson from Michigan in the second round of the 2004 NBA draft, my second year in the league. The 2004-2005 TWCA team was improved with another trip to the state tournament and district title, this time making it to the state semifinals. We had turned this program into a consistent winner posting a two-year record of 50-10. Derek was continuing to flourish and was getting recognition from college coaches. People in the community were noticing what we were doing at the school. We had won more games than ever before, against a tough schedule of both private and public schools. The talent level was rising as more players were coming to be a part of it. Joe Carr, who had played with the HCYA home school team in Houston was our best new player. Joe came from a great family, was an honor student, and was one of the fiercest competitors I had ever seen. With the addition of Carr, we had a chance to do something special at the school. Derek and Joe had played together on our summer team, Houston Select. They had become close friends and gave us a 1-2 punch like no other team in the metro. Other players came as well, and we now had solid players at every position as well as depth at each spot.

 I now considered myself a veteran on the NBA scouting circuit, and there were stories from the road that could easily fill an encyclopedia. One of which was after scouting at the Big East Tournament in New York. After watching a four-overtime game between Syracuse and Connecticut at Madison Square Garden that went late into the night, I caught an early morning flight to Cincinnati for the Atlantic 10 tourney. This was just a couple of years after the 9-11 tragedy, and I was flying a small twin prop commuter plane from LaGuardia to Cincinnati. This was before the FAA had secured cockpit doors on small commercial aircraft. We were in mid-flight to Cincinnati when I felt a hand from behind me grab my arm. It was an off-duty flight attendant who was asking for my help with an unruly passenger. As I turned around, I saw a man walking towards the front of the plane with his hands clenched together and formed like a gun and screaming that he was flying this plane into the White House. The flight attendant then went into the cockpit to inform the pilots of the problem. There was only a curtain that separated the passengers from the pilots and if this man got into the cockpit we were in serious trouble. The plane began a sharp descent, and the man kept walking forward and yelling out ... this time he was screaming something about a known terrorist group. I was sitting in seat 1A, the last seat before getting to the cockpit area. I stood up, as did my fellow passenger in seat 1B. We formed sort of a blockade across the aisle and implored the passenger to return to his seat. He kept coming. The passenger in 1B was a big guy and I stand around 6'6. The other passenger kept screaming and kept coming towards the cockpit until he got to us. 1B had taken off his belt to use as a weapon if needed. We again implored the problem passenger to go back to his seat, but he screamed out and took a swing at 1B. We jumped on top of him in the aisle with about five or six other passengers while the plane was on a steep descent. We had him subdued until the plane landed after diverting to Columbus. The descent was so hard, fast, and steep that we blew a tire on impact with the runway in Columbus. As soon as we came to a stop the exit door flung open and FBI agents began swarming the plane with weapons drawn. All the passengers went into the terminal to be interviewed and were held up for several hours. I called the office in Charlotte to let them know what had happened and received half-hearted accolades from the staff for "saving America." I was late to the Atlantic 10 tournament and after the games watched the news on TV that reported a "disturbance" on a commuter flight from New York to Cincinnati. We laugh about it now, but it could have been a serious thing. Turned out the passenger was not at all a terrorist, but rather a man with a history of mental illness who hadn't taken his medication. He was released and I got a $600 travel voucher from the airline for "giving aid in a situation that could have had severe consequences." This was sometimes the life of an NBA scout ... so many games, so many flights, so many hotel rooms, and so many stories that never get told.

In 2006 Michael Jordan became a minority owner of the Bobcats and managing member of basketball operations. In essence, he became my boss and was in charge of pretty much everything on the basketball side of the organization. Kenny Williamson was still my direct supervisor, but Jordan was calling the shots. MJ was truly bigger than life in the eyes of most basketball fans and probably the greatest player to ever play the game. I met him for the first time during the 2006 NBA draft in Charlotte and was absolutely starstruck. One of the first things I noticed is whenever he walked into a setting, he instantly became the smartest, funniest, most handsome guy in the room. It wasn't really true of course, but it seemed that way, and it was rare that anyone had the gumption to disagree with our new boss. He was, after all, the greatest ever. In 2006 with Jordan leading the way, we drafted Adam Morrison from Gonzaga with the number three pick in the first round. Morrison turned out to be one of the biggest busts in NBA draft history and never made a significant contribution to the Bobcats or anyone else. To be fair, Morrison had type one diabetes and tore an ACL in his second year in the league. But it became one of the biggest draft regrets of the Charlotte organization.

After the NBA draft, I returned home and spent another summer with Derek traveling with Houston Select. He had a great summer and was already getting recruiting letters from college coaches after his sophomore year at TWCA. We were excited about the upcoming season and knew we had a championship-caliber team. TWCA had also changed its head administrator during the past year. John Echols was gone and replaced by local businesswoman Julie Ambler. I didn't know Ambler, but she was a TWCA parent with kids currently enrolled at the school and seemed legitimately interested in continuing to grow as a school. I was called in for a meeting with her after the 2007 season. Ambler and the board had an idea. During the meeting, it became clear that the board wanted to expand my role at the school as athletic director over all sports. I was already working full-time as an NBA scout and as the school's basketball coach. But Ambler assured me that adding this role would not interfere with either. At this point, I just wanted to help in any way possible. I held great affection for the school, and it gave me what I needed to have a successful basketball program. I accepted the job and became the new TWCA athletic director.

Scheduling high school games becomes more difficult when you have a reputation for having a good team. Most of the public-school coaches didn't want to risk losing to a small, private school so they just wouldn't play us. We took all-comers and a few of the big schools stepped up. I have always felt like playing against better competition would only make my team better. The Bobcats trusted me now to make my own travel and game schedule, so I did my best to be home for most of the TWCA games. I had great confidence in Coach Storey and the team never missed a beat when I was gone. The team steamrolled through the 2007-2008 season with another district championship and a 21-2 record heading into our third straight state tournament. Derek and Joe Carr were great together as I knew they would be, and we were the favorites going into the final four in San Antonio. Expectations had been high all season and our guys played to their potential every night. Going into the Final Four I was more nervous than I had ever been before a game. But this wasn't about me at all. I wanted these kids to experience what it was like to win it all. Their families had trusted in me enough to pay a hefty tuition to TWCA in order for their son to be a part of something special. We were making history and making memories, and the pressure I put on myself was astounding. We prayed before every game as a team, and I prayed constantly. I've never asked God to help us win a game, just that His will be done, that we would play our best, that we would stay clear of injury, and that we would honor Him with our efforts. I know lots of coaches and others pray to win in all walks of life and I guess that's ok. I just never felt quite right about asking God to let us win a basketball game. But if I was ever tempted, this would be the time.

  We won easily in the state semifinals and would play for the state championship the next day against Kingwood Christian. We were clearly a better team than Kingwood and had already defeated them twice during the regular season. People say it's hard to beat a team three times in a season. I've always taken a different approach thinking that if you're good enough to win twice against a team, you should be good enough to win a third time. In any event, our guys were confident, and Kingwood had to question their ability to beat us since they had never done it. On March 2, 2008, we dominated the game, and TWCA won its first-ever state championship in any sport by a score of 70-52. It seemed our entire school was at the game, and our guys were ecstatic. For me, it was mostly a relief. This is what we had set out to do. Three years earlier the school had never experienced a winning season in basketball and today, we were State Champions. I was happiest for our kids, their families, and our school. But there was some personal satisfaction as well after all that had happened. And maybe the greatest satisfaction I will ever know was being a part of Derek's life and watching him achieve. He would never forget this moment.

We celebrated with an all-school assembly when we returned to The Woodlands, complete with the raising of the championship trophy, recognition of our players, and a prayer of gratitude. I was a proud coach and a proud dad. In the stands, I watched younger students at the school that looked at our current players with adoring eyes. I could see their hopes and dreams of being on that stage themselves someday. We were experiencing a change in culture, where winning with honor became the story. God's hand was in all of this. And with the majority of our team back again next year, we might be able to do it again.

"Do not remember the former things, nor consider the things of old. Behold I will do a new thing, now shall it spring forth." Isaiah 43:18

CHAPTER 19 - BACK-TO-BACK (AGAIN)

After the tournament, I was back on the road for the Bobcats finishing another season of evaluation. With Michael Jordan now in the fold, we were bound to make significant changes, especially in personnel. The first big shoe to drop was the resignation of our general manager and head coach, Bernie Bickerstaff. I absolutely loved Bernie … he had been an NBA legend, was a great coach and boss, and was one of the smartest men I knew. Michael hired Larry Brown to replace him as head coach, who was obviously a legendary coach in his own right. MJ's best friend, Rod Higgins, was hired as general manager. In the 2008 draft, we selected DJ Augustin, a point guard from the University of Texas with the number nine pick in the first round, and Alexis Ajinca, from France in the second round. Ajinca was a favorite of new coach Larry Brown but was probably not the guy the scouting staff would have selected. Augustin was an undersized point guard by NBA standards but was a solid pick and had a long career in the league.

After the draft, I came home to Houston for Derek's last summer of AAU basketball. I had been his summer coach as well as his high school coach, and I thought this would be a good time to start letting go of the reins. I stepped aside as coach of Houston Select and asked Coach Todd Smith to take over. Smith had been an assistant coach at Rice University and had just been hired as coach at St. Thomas University in Houston. Smith was a great coach and took over to get involved in the Houston area high school AAU basketball scene and hopefully gain an advantage in recruiting Houston area kids for St. Thomas. Derek and Joe Carr were in good hands with Coach Smith, and their final summer of travel team basketball was memorable. Both were being recruited at the division one level and made a good showing on the summer circuit in 2008. Personnel shakeups for the Bobcats continued after the draft and into the summer. MJ obviously wanted to put his stamp on the organization and brought in some of his own hires. I received a call from Kenny Williamson late in the summer about a shake-up within the organization. Kenny explained that Michael wanted to overhaul the college scouting department and would be making some changes. This didn't sound good, and I held my breath as he told me that they were letting all of the current scouts go ... except for me. I was never quite sure why I made the cut, and I hated losing some of my Bobcat teammates but was grateful I still had a job. But rumors continued to swirl in Charlotte and a short time after the call, Williamson accepted a position with the Memphis Grizzlies. Kenny had been my mentor and was the guy that brought me into the NBA. We had become more than co-workers. He was a trusted friend and a guy who I will always remember with fondness and gratitude. Eggman, as he was affectionately known, took me under his wing and showed me the NBA ropes. Kenny took the Memphis job as a promotion and was a major part of their rebuild. But Kenny was diagnosed with cancer shortly after taking the Grizzlies job and died in 2012. Kenny "Eggman" Williamson was 65 years old when he passed. I'll never forget him, and I thank God that our paths crossed.

  We started back to school in August 2008, and it would be Derek's final year of high school. By now he had received scholarship offers from USC, Colorado, Evansville, Middle Tennessee and several others. Denna and I made a couple of recruiting visits with him, and we went together on his visit to Middle Tennessee. They were in the mix mostly because head coach Kermit Davis was a good friend, and his new assistant coach was Win Case, my former assistant at OCU. The early signing period was in November and Derek wanted recruiting to be over with so he could focus on his senior year and trying to win another state championship. After taking several official visits, he signed with the University of Evansville in Indiana who was a member of the Missouri Valley Conference. Joe Carr signed with VMI (Virginia Military Institute) and now it was time to concentrate on the upcoming season. We had added a couple more key players over the summer, and we were loaded. Preseason rankings had us ranked #1 in our statewide classification, and #1 in Montgomery County which included a number of both public and private schools. We were all looking forward to the season and in my mind, it would likely be my last year at TWCA. Derek would be graduating, and I had a little girl who lived in Oklahoma City that needed more attention from her dad. Unless God had other plans and something drastic happened, I would be headed back to Oklahoma after graduation. The Bobcats didn't care where I lived at this point, and I needed to become a bigger part of my daughter's life. Kenny Williamson had been replaced by Scott Howard for Charlotte and Howard had previously worked with Michael in the Washington Wizards organization. Scott was a longtime friend dating back to our college coaching days and I could not be happier to be working with him. The heat was getting ready to get turned way up as I headed into Derek's senior year at TWCA, faced the pressure of repeating as state champs, embracing my job as head coach and athletic director at the school, and working with a new regime in Charlotte. It was a lot, and I was grateful. God's blessings continued.

Part of my scouting job included going to live college practices once they started up in October. So, the preseason was busy with both college and TWCA practice sessions, my duties as athletic director, home football games, and making out my season schedule for scouting and travel. There was a buzz around campus once the season rolled around with expectations that were through the roof. Nothing short of another state championship would be acceptable to me or the players on our team. And we started the season on a roll in dominating fashion. We were playing mostly against bigger schools and any public school that would play us. We won our fourth straight district championship en route to the final four, this time to be played in Mansfield. We brought a record of 30-4 with us to the semifinals, but all of a sudden, we had some major problems to overcome. Joe Carr, our second-leading scorer had a sprained right ankle and was only playing at about fifty percent. Derek had a bad left ankle sprain that would likely keep him out of the semifinal game. The two had combined for an average of more than thirty points and fifteen rebounds per game over the course of the season. With our top two players in limbo, our chances of a repeat seemed in serious jeopardy. Our first opponent in Mansfield was Arlington Christian Academy. Carr was healthy enough to play but would be considerably less than a hundred percent. Derek was out with a swollen ankle the size of a grapefruit. He pleaded with me to let him play in the semifinals, but it was too risky. If we could somehow get by our first-round opponent, we would re-evaluate his availability for the state championship game. Carr and small forward Evan Flance were terrific in the semifinal game, and we broke the game open late for a 55-39 victory. We would play the next day for the state championship against Fort Worth Christian.

The big question was obviously whether Derek would be able to play in the state finals. He had been getting treatments all week and the swelling in his left ankle had subsided some. He wanted to play in the worst way ... and it had all come down to this. It would be the final game of his high school career, playing for a repeat state championship on a bum ankle. It would likely be the last game I would ever coach at TWCA or maybe anywhere else. He was walking with a noticeable limp, and I didn't see any way he could run or jump. But there would be no tomorrow and no second chance. The game tipped off and Derek was in the starting lineup.

Derek's first shot in the game was a three-pointer that missed everything ... an air ball. He was pressing and as much as he wanted to play in this game, we both knew he would be limited. I substituted frequently to try and keep his minutes down. But once he settled in, he was effective. And the substitutions weren't helping. Time on the bench just caused the ankle to stiffen. I decided to just let him play. Derek scored a couple of baskets from close range, but he was most valuable on the defensive end and was guarding their best player. We held a slim lead with just a few minutes left to play and I signaled from the bench to go into our delay game. There was no shot clock in high school basketball so I thought that with our two best players injured, our best chance would be to try and run out the clock. But Derek hadn't seen the call from the bench and on the next possession he let fly on a three-pointer trailing on a fast break. It was an ill-advised shot at the most critical point in the state championship game. But the shot went in and it broke open the game and gave us a cushion. We finished in our delay game and shot nothing but layups and free throws the rest of the way. The buzzer sounded and we had won back-to-back state championships with a 49-38 victory over Fort Worth Christian. Derek led us in scoring with 14 points on a severely sprained ankle, but we had so many players contribute in a big way. It was the culmination of four years at the school ending with an overall record of 109-16, with four straight district championships and two state championships. And the best part was that I went through all of it with my son. The success, the championships, the time spent with Derek, the friendships made, the NBA job, and getting my life back on the right path could all be traced back to one single event. It was the day I said yes to God and followed him in obedience.

The celebration began after the buzzer sounded. Derek and I

hugged at half-court, and that photo still hangs in my office. Two days later I informed TWCA that I would not be returning after this school year. It had been the best four years of my life with a spiritual growth that I had never known before. God had fulfilled his promise that he would never leave nor forsake me. This was not major college or professional basketball. It was a small high school program in Texas, that had experienced an unbelievable turnaround because of God's grace. It would be silly for me or anyone else to take credit for any of this. This was God's handiwork pure and simple. The last game I ever coached at Baylor University was at Reunion Arena in Dallas with a capacity crowd of 19,000. The last game I ever coached at TWCA was in a small high school gym in front of a crowd estimated at around 900. But in my experience, I've found that the thing about most coaches is that once that ball goes up in the air it doesn't much matter where we are or who's watching. We don't really care about the level of competition, the notoriety or the press clippings. We're here because we love the game, and we just want to help kids be successful. We all definitely want to win, but in the end, it's more about the relationships that we've formed and helping players become the best they can be. I said it to my players a thousand times … there are more important things in life than being a good basketball player, but there's nothing more important than being the best you can become. But life's most important lesson that had evaded me for so long was that there's nothing more important or more fulfilling, than walking through life in God's purpose. A few days later TWCA submitted a press release that I was leaving the school, and I gave thanks to all who had contributed to our success. Our school principal, Steve Zeal was quoted in the Houston Chronicle on March 2, 2009,

"Coach Johnson has been a tremendous service to the school which goes beyond wins and losses. He has turned boys, not just into good basketball players, but into great young men."

A wonderful complement from Zeal, but really I had just been the vehicle, that had been used for the glory of Jesus Christ. It was ultimately what TWCA was all about, and finally what I had become.

"But those who trust in the Lord will find new strength. They will soar high on wings like eagles. They will run and not grow weary."
Isaiah 40:31

CHAPTER 20 - THE BUZZER SOUNDS

Derek graduated early from TWCA to get a head start with workouts at the University of Evansville, presumably his home for the next four years. He was awarded the Montgomery County Player of the Year, and I was voted the Coach of the Year. The headlines in the local newspaper read, "It's A Family Affair." And that pretty much sums it up. I recommended Bill Storey as my successor, and he was hired. I was confident the program at TWCA was in good hands. As planned, I moved back to Oklahoma City and continued working for the Bobcats. In 2010 Michael Jordan bought the majority stake in the team for 275 million dollars, a paltry sum by today's standards. He continued bringing in new people and I continued to love my NBA scouting career.

In 2010 we had another lottery pick at number twelve, and Jordan had his eyes set on Terrence Williams from Louisville. He was a bit rough around the edges but a super-talented athlete, nonetheless. As we always do, we had done extensive background work on each prospective draftable player, as well as gathered intel from other teams. We weren't sure if Williams would be available at #12, so we began trying to find out who the teams ahead of us in the draft might take. All of us had our sources, and there were some more reliable than others. It's amazing every year around the draft how much misinformation is put out by teams. Part of the job is to find out what's real and what isn't. Jordan had all of us contact our sources to see who was on the radar for each team. We were picking at #12 and the New Jersey (now Brooklyn) Nets held the pick ahead of us at #11. I had great sources within the Nets organization and began calling them. The word I was getting was that the Nets planned to select Terrence Williams at eleven. The information was reliable, from sources that had never let me down before. But I also had information that they were not exactly enamored with Williams and would have an interest in trading down. One of my closest friends in the Nets organizations told me flat out that they would swap picks with us if we would throw in a future second-round pick. It was a way for MJ to get his man if that's who he really wanted, for a throwaway future second round pick. It was draft day with all of us in the Charlotte draft room utilizing the phones trying to get solid intel. I hung up with the Nets and announced my information to Michael saying it came from reliable sources. Everyone in the room got quiet waiting to see if Michael would do the deal. His answer was that he knew for a fact that Rod Thorn (Nets team president) would not draft Terrence Williams. He told me, and others in the room that Thorn was the guy that had drafted him in Chicago and that Williams was not a Rod Thorn-type player. Basically, he was saying that my information was wrong. I argued ... saying that this source was a trusted and reliable friend who had never given me bad information. He argued back again that Rod Thorn would never draft a player like Terrence Williams, and the Nets were just using me to try and extort a future pick from us. Jordan was the boss, so I politely deferred. I had given my opinion, which was my job, and it was possible that Jordan was absolutely right. There have been times when upper-level team executives would give misinformation to their own staff, just in case someone was giving away information. I was a scout, and it was my job to offer evaluations and suggestions, not to make decisions. We stood pat at number twelve and watched the draft as it was unfolding, with the Nets taking Terrence Williams with their pick at eleven. I was vindicated but Jordan seemed embarrassed. Instead, we took Gerald Henderson from Duke with our pick at twelve, which was probably a hard thing for Michael to do being a former North Carolina player. No one ever talked about what had happened in the draft room that night, but at the end of the summer when my contract was up for renewal I was let go by the Bobcats. The notification came as a "courtesy call" from Rod Higgins, our general manager, saying my contract was not being renewed due to budget cuts. I could never prove it, but I believe my tenure in Charlotte was cut short because my draft information had correctly contradicted Michael's beliefs that the Nets were not going to take the guy we wanted. Terrence Williams never panned out for the Nets and didn't last long in the NBA, and Gerald Henderson had a decent career with Charlotte but never helped them get to a higher level. My career in Charlotte ended because I had done my job well. At least that's what I believed. I phoned my boss in Charlotte, Scott

Howard, letting him know what had happened. He had no idea and didn't see it coming. He agreed that it had nothing to do with budget cuts since the team had likely spent more on the staff Christmas party than on my salary. Scott was an extremely loyal friend and vowed to help me stay employed with another NBA team.

Experience in this profession was my strongest suit, and I had networked while working for six years for the Bobcats, making lots of friends and acquaintances. Pretty quickly and with Scott's help, I caught on with the New Orleans Hornets, who later became the Pelicans. The job was mostly the same as I had been doing with the Bobcats but was more regional in scope than nationwide. I was back in Oklahoma City now with Derek off to college in Evansville. I already knew several of the New Orleans staffers and quickly made friends with others. My supervisor would be Gerald Madkins, who had played for UCLA and in the NBA with several different teams. He was also an experienced NBA executive with multiple teams. Gerald and I hit it off almost immediately, and he would become a great friend and confidant. But Madkins became frustrated in New Orleans after a couple of years and took a job back home in Los Angeles with the Clippers as assistant general manager. We drafted well during my time in New Orleans, acquiring guys like Anthony Davis and Buddy Hield in the lottery and several other solid role players. Tim Connelly, our assistant GM in New Orleans also left the organization to become the new general manager for the Denver Nuggets and hired my old boss in Charlotte, Scott Howard. Soon after, I got an opportunity to work with Gerald again with the Clippers and jumped at the chance. So, after five-plus years in New Orleans, I was now a Clipper and felt excited and refreshed about the new position. The Clips were undergoing changes themselves with Doc Rivers giving up his front office duties as GM but remaining as head coach. New owner Steve Balmer felt strongly that the job should be split and tabbed long-time coach Lawrence Frank as the new President of Basketball Operations. Frank had no experience as an NBA executive, but the guy was an absolute workaholic and quickly made the transition. He had put together a first-rate scouting staff of experienced evaluation experts, and with Ballmer as owner, he was given the resources to build a world-class organization. The organization in New Orleans had been somewhat dysfunctional under the leadership of GM Dell Demps, especially compared to our first group in Charlotte which had been stellar. But the Clippers were in a class by themselves. They had everything covered with exceptional leadership from ownership on down. I've often said that the Clippers might not have the best team, but it could very well be the best professional sports organization in the world. The job in L.A. was demanding and I was on the road more than ever before. I loved our Clippers group, but Madkins left the team in 2017 to go back to the New York Knicks where he had previously worked. It was a step up for Gerald, but I hated to see him go. We drafted Shai Gilgeous-Alexander from Kentucky in 2018 and traded him for Kawhi Leonard and Paul George in 2019. The move was mostly seen as a huge success for the Clippers franchise and made the team an instant contender for an NBA championship. For his part in the move, Lawrence Frank received NBA Executive of the Year honors in 2020. Ballmer fired Doc Rivers after the 2020 season and assistant coach Ty Lue took over. We had our best season in franchise history in 2021 with newly acquired stars Kawhi Leonard and Paul George leading the way to the Western Conference Finals. Leonard went down in game five with a torn ACL and we were eliminated by the Suns in game six. Had Leonard not gotten injured, the Clippers had a legitimate chance to become NBA champions in 2021. But it was not to be. Kawhi's injury problems continued, and George was eventually traded. Gilgeous-Alexander has become an NBA star in Oklahoma City while leading his team to the 2025 NBA championship and receiving the league's MVP award. The job and the travel were taking a toll on my sixty-seven-year-old body and in 2022 I retired after 20 years in the NBA. I had become active in my daughter's life in Oklahoma City, and she was living with me after graduating from the University of Oklahoma. I had been inconsistently present in Lauren's early life but had done my best to keep a good relationship going, even with the distance between us. It was challenging, to say the least, and she made a lot of basketball trips with her dad in those early days. Derek left Evansville after a major knee injury that required two big surgeries. He transferred to NCAA Division Two member Oklahoma Christian, which was just a few minutes from where I lived. It was great having Derek close by again, but he was becoming frustrated with the game after his surgeries left him less physically able to be the player he had been before the injury. He stayed at OC for the next 3 years and then moved back to Texas to finish his degree. I also met a new lady in Oklahoma City that I wanted to have a future with. Beth and I had actually met and become friends in 2018 but had now progressed to the point of being in a committed relationship. She had also been married before, and we brought all of our experiences and baggage to the relationship. But what was different this time around was that we were both committed to keeping God first in our lives and in our relationship. In October of 2022, we married. Beth and I currently lead a small group through our church called Marriage 2.0. It's a couple's group for those who have lost a spouse to death or divorce and have a blended family. It's been one of the great blessings in our lives to go through life with like-minded friends that live by faith.

Retirement is challenging for sure and in the spring of 2023, Beth and I were vacationing in Florida when I received a phone call from Gerald Madkins. Gerald had retired a couple of years earlier from his job with the New York Knicks, so I assumed it was a call to mostly just catch up. Not only had we worked together with the Pelicans and the Clippers, but our relationship went beyond that into a close friendship and mutual respect. Gerald had received some interest from the front office of the Phoenix Suns about an executive position within the organization. He would become the Vice President for Personnel Evaluation with the Suns and asked me to come with him. The Suns were lagging way behind the rest of the league in terms of their player personnel evaluation, without any real system in place. Gerald explained that there was very little experience in the front office and needed an experienced staff to get headed in the right direction. New owner Matt Ishbia had made waves in free agency with the addition of Kevin Durant and Bradley Beal, but the team hadn't particularly drafted well in recent years. Madkins painted a pretty enticing picture of the new job. It would basically be a short-term position for a year or two, to mentor some of the younger scouts and help implement a standardized scouting system. My job would be the responsibility of identifying and evaluating draft prospects in the South and Southeast regions of the country, but Gerald would give me complete autonomy as to how to best do the job. It was based on a level of trust that had developed between us after working side by side for seven years, in two different organizations. He asked me to consider coming out of retirement and to take a couple of weeks to think it through. We would not have any responsibilities for the 2023 draft, but the job would begin with the 2023-2024 college season. I had gotten acclimated to a life of retirement, but this was sort of a dream job opportunity and working with one of my best friends. I would make my own travel schedule and could see as many or as few live games as I thought was necessary. Gerald made it pretty clear that my responsibilities for the position would be entirely self implemented, and that I would only answer to him. The call lasted for a couple of hours and Beth had been with me the entire time. She only heard one side of the conversation but had deduced what was going on. The call ended and I looked straight at her. She was smiling … and saw the feeble attempt to feign my excitement. It was flattering to be pursued but the biggest draw to me was the opportunity to work with Gerald. Beth and I prayed about it, felt led, and accepted the job with Phoenix. My official title was Senior Evaluation Analyst, and my duties were exactly as Madkins had described. The team and staff assembled at summer league in Las Vegas, and then again at training camp in Phoenix. We were all excited about the opportunities that we'd been given, and to work for a team that most thought would be an NBA contender. But the optimism was short-lived as the team underachieved and the Suns were the most dysfunctional organization I had been with. I find it unlikely the Suns will ever be a factor again in the NBA race unless major changes are made in the leadership. But I enjoyed the year getting reacquainted with colleagues and working with Madkins. But we only lasted one season. Gerald left the organization, and I retired again. I won't be surprised if Gerald makes another run with another NBA team at some point … because there's no one better in the business than Gerald Madkins. But I'm retired for good this time. After a lifetime of basketball, the ups and downs of coaching and NBA scouting, the time had come to let go and call it a career. I left the game that I loved so dearly in the summer of 2024 with a heart of gratitude and thankfulness. The buzzer has sounded.

"They will still bear fruit in old age; they will stay fresh and green."
Psalm 92:14

CHAPTER 21 – REFLECTIONS

It's Only a Game has been a work in progress for decades and has proved to be a bittersweet journey. Having sought advice from authors, friends, and colleagues for years before attempting it, the same question kept repeating itself. Why write a book? The consensus seemed to be that before commencing this adventure, I should try and determine its purpose. But the purpose has evolved with each passing season of life. There have been stages of grief, joy, anger, heartache, and laughter throughout the writing. Beth has traveled some of the road with me, especially during the past year while putting it all together. She's been nothing but supportive, understanding, encouraging, and loving through it all. There were stories that brought back memories of both tears and celebration. But I've determined that my purpose in writing It's Only a Game is multi-faceted. First is the fact that the true story has never been told publicly. When John O'Dell asked me to speak at a retired coaches luncheon in January 2024, I felt that old divine nudge again. It was like God was saying … it's time. After all, it's only been thirty years since the Baylor trial. My experience tells me to always "trust the nudge." So, I write first and foremost as an act of Godly obedience. He gave me the story, and now it was finally time to tell it. I have a great friend, Kent Shellenberger, who encouraged me to tell the story, even if it helps only one other person who might be fighting the most difficult of life challenges. Maybe my story could help, encourage, inspire, or even point others toward Jesus. It's my hope that others can learn some valuable life lessons from reading this book. Because I learned two critical lessons in my journey that I believe will serve all of us as we travel down life's road. The first would be that one single act of obedience to God can change the entire trajectory of your life. I had fought and argued with God about leaving Oklahoma City and going to Houston. I wasn't keen on giving up my plan and facing the unknown where I had little or no control over the outcome. Even after the act of obeying God, I still tried to control the ending. But then came the second greatest lesson.

That God's plan is always better than ours. I was hoping to finish a career in basketball in a small Texas town with the most foolproof plan that was derived from an act of Godly obedience. But He had a different plan. One that was beyond what I could possibly have dreamed about or hoped for. If I hadn't "trusted the nudge" and answered God's call to just go, I would have missed out on His perfect plan. I would have missed out on twenty-one years of dream jobs with four different NBA teams. I would have missed out on coaching my son and being a part of his everyday life. I would have missed out on coaching two state championships with Derek, which became the crowning achievement of my entire professional life. It's been my experience that we tend to think much smaller than God does. I did my best to make a complete mess of things in my personal life and career when all I ever needed to do was give it all to Him. Once I surrendered to Him, everything fell into place and God's perfect plan was executed.

There will be those who question the purpose of authoring this book. It will likely be suggested or inferred by some that it is for financial gain or self-promotion. But any proceeds from It's Only a Game are to be donated to faith-based charities. I am blessed to be covered by the provisions of God and feel compelled now to give back. I've also been motivated to tell my story since it has been obliterated throughout the years with untruths and factually incorrect information. Then there is the notion that It's Only a Game is about self-promotion or spinning the story in a favorable light. But in truth, the hardships, difficulties, and supreme challenges in my life have been, for the most part, self-induced. At the same time, I take no credit or claims of responsibility that have resulted in the good that has happened, or the life-changing climb out of the depths of despair and hurt. The turnaround and upward transformation in my life has all been facilitated by the grace of God, and the result of putting my complete trust in Him.

Since I began giving my testimony and telling my story in 2024, I'm sometimes asked if I have regrets, or if I would change anything if I could go back. The regrets I have surround others who were harmed along the way. I wish I hadn't made Denna a single mom. She deserved better and was the one person in my life that I hurt the most. She's now in a wonderful place in life, is a great friend to me, and has been gracious and forgiving for all my transgressions that caused her pain. My son is fortunate to have the best mom I could ever want for him, and Denna's entire life has been a great example of faith and walking with Christ. Children of divorce are often faced with difficulties that they play no part in creating. In spite of all that has happened, my son and daughter are leading blessed lives of their own, though I wish I could have spared them the inner turmoil of becoming children of divorce. I wish I hadn't brought in assistant coaches to an environment at Baylor where we had almost no chance to succeed. They became convicted felons through little fault of their own, and I believe were wrongly accused of federal crimes. It appears they've all rebounded nicely, and I hope they've found their own inner peace and faith in God. I regret that our players at Baylor didn't get to participate in an NCAA tournament or compete for championships. Most of them were the most innocent of victims and didn't deserve the punishment they received. But I'll never regret the hard times and brokenness of what transpired in my life. There are some of us who have to face great loss and challenges to learn life's lessons and to ultimately become what God wants us to be. Through the years, I've learned that every storm is a school, every trial is a teacher, and every experience is an education. It's been said that life on earth is God's gift to us, and what we do with it is our gift to God. None of us want to be judged by the worst decisions we've made in our life, or the struggles that we've created for ourselves. The person I've become today is one who loves Jesus more than anything else, and is a product of the experiences, both good and difficult, that He's given me. I am eternally grateful for both. I have no hard feelings towards anyone, and I enter the fourth quarter of life with a heart of overwhelming gratitude. As I look back, I hope my life is not defined by my failures. But I also hope that it's not judged by my successes. I've had plenty of both. My story is not really my story at all. It all belongs to God and it's not about championships, winning games, awards and accolades, or twenty-one years in the NBA. This story is about the grace, the forgiveness, the mercy and the redemption of Jesus Christ. Scripture says in James 1, "Blessed are those that persevere through trials, having stood the test, that they shall receive the crown of life, that the Lord has promised to those that love Him."

And that right there … is my championship.

ABOUT THE AUTHOR

Darrel Johnson's career spans over four decades of transformative leadership in basketball, education, and service. Beginning as a high school coach in Ada, Oklahoma, he quickly rose through the collegiate ranks, serving as assistant coach at Oklahoma State before leading programs at Oklahoma Baptist, Oklahoma City University—where he won two national championships and earned two National Coach of the Year honors—and Baylor University. His coaching excellence was recognized with five Conference Coach of the Year awards and Hall of Fame inductions at both Oklahoma City University and Putnam City High School. Transitioning into athletic administration, he served as Athletic Director at Woodlands Christian High School while also leading Home At Last Inc., a real estate initiative focused on community development. Johnson then embarked on a 20-year NBA career in scouting and player personnel, contributing to the Charlotte Bobcats, New Orleans Pelicans, LA Clippers, and Phoenix Suns. In 2024, he retired from professional basketball and now serves as President and Chairman of the Board of WTL Adventures, a nonprofit dedicated to faith-based mentorship.

Other titles from Higher Ground Books & Media:

The Children's Bread by Terra Kern

God's Whispers by Christine Nekas Thoma

Meant to Be by Becka L. Jones

Of Life and Automobiles by Frank Adkins

Shameless Persistence by Sandra Bretting

Finding Purpose in the Pain by Brenda W. McIntyre

Hush: Breaking the Chains of Abuse by Yasmin S. Brown

Raven Transcending Fear by Terri Kozlowski

The Real Prison Diaries by Judy Frisby

Bits & Pieces by Rebecca Whited

One Day in May by Joanne Piccari Coleman

Through the Sliver of a Frosted Window by Robin Melet

Full Gospel by Rev. Jerry C. Crossley

Chronicles of a Spiritual Journey by Stephen Shepherd

Don't Be Stupid (And I Mean That in the Nicest Way) by Rebecca Benston

Add these titles to your collection today!

http://www.highergroundbooksandmedia.com

HIGHER GROUND BOOKS & MEDIA IS AN INDEPENDENT PUBLISHER

Do you have a story to tell?

Higher Ground Books & Media is an independent Christian-based publisher specializing in stories of triumph! Our purpose is to empower, inspire, and educate through the sharing of personal experiences.

We are always looking for great new stories to add to our collection. If you're looking for a publisher, get in touch with us today!

Please be sure to visit our website for our submission guidelines.

http://www.highergroundbooksandmedia.com/submission-guidelines

AUTHOR SERVICES

HGBM Services offers a variety of writing and coaching services for aspiring authors! We can help with editing, manuscript critiques, self-publishing, and much more! Get in touch today to see how we can help you make your dream of becoming an author a reality!

http://www.highergroundbooksandmedia.com/editing-writing-services

Need Bulk Copies?

If you would like to order bulk copies of this book or any other title at Higher Ground Books & Media, please contact us at highergroundbooksandmedia@gmail.com.

We offer discounts for purchases of 20 or more copies. Excellent for small groups, book clubs, classrooms, etc.

Get in touch today and get a set of great stories for your students or group members.

www.ingramcontent.com/pod-product-compliance
Lightning Source LLC
Chambersburg PA
CBHW060517100426
42743CB00009B/1355